My Last Drink, the Greatest Human Story Ever Written; a Powerful Personal History of a Chicago Alderman and Well-known Business man who Dropped From Power and Wealth to Poverty and Prison Through Drink

MY
LAST DRINK

THE GREATEST HUMAN STORY
EVER WRITTEN

A powerful personal history of a Chicago
Alderman and well-known business man
who dropped from power and wealth to
poverty and prison through drink.

By Alderman JOSEPH H. FRANCIS, Chicago

A Tragic History that Every Man and Woman
in America Should Read

Published by
THE EMPIRE BOOK CO.,
633 Plymouth Court
CHICAGO

THE MODERN PRESS, CHICAGO

NOTICE

IF YOU are unable to purchase

"MY LAST DRINK"

at your local bookstore or from your news-
dealer, a copy will be sent, postpaid, on
receipt of Fifty Cents by the publishers—

THE EMPIRE BOOK COMPANY,
633 Plymouth Court,
CHICAGO, ILL.
Telephone—Harrison 5321.

❈ FRANCISGRAMS ❈

Booze boycotts the brain.

A boozer has a dent in his brain.

A little drink makes a big man shrink.

All saloon keepers argue that a fly is a pest.

Take a pony of brandy and ride to destruction.

A boozer may fool himself, but he cannot fool nature.

Battling with booze is like trying to corner the wind.

A saloon keeper's friendship is tied with a rope of sand.

Drinking men are the architects of their own misfortunes.

You don't find comfort or prosperity in the home of a booze fighter.

Some men's idea of pleasure is to do the things that brings them misery.

When you see a prominent citizen trying to unlock his front door with a lead pencil, look out.

The only man in the universe that can get full and keep his head with him is the man in the moon.

FRANCISGRAMS

Whiskey and war are twins.

Booze is the best stranger in the world.

Moderation in drinking is damnation in embryo.

A saloon keeper is simply a stoker for the devil.

Booze is the misery of many for the gain of a few.

A glass of booze is a ticket in the lottery of death.

Let us crush these booze artists in human slaughter.

A lazy man never kicks when carrying a heavy load of booze.

A saloon keeper floats the American flag and hands you a shroud.

If you want to pluck the flower of sorrow follow the booze route.

A corkscrew is straight compared with the average saloon keeper.

Field of honor for sober men, Potter's field for drinking men.

A saloon keeper's friendship is like the tide; when you are all in, he's out.

FRANCISGRAMS

Safety first is sobriety first.

Gin and genius make a faulty team.

A whiskey smile soon turns to a frown.

Alcohol is not included in the scheme of life.

What is a chaser? Ask the snake in the whiskey.

It is only a short life from the Blackstone to the Bridewell.

Whiskey is the monkey wrench in the machinery of efficiency.

The saloons do not need regulation, they need strangulation.

A street car says:—"Pay as you enter." A saloon, "Die as you enter."

A saloon thrives on widows' tears, mothers' heartaches and starving children.

An old man with white hair is today more in demand than a young man with a red nose.

Split a bottle of champagne with a saloon keeper and he will usually reciprocate by splitting a bottle of beer.

FRANCISGRAMS

Thinkers are not drinkers.

Booze has no place in business.

Good intentions never enter saloon doors.

Every "day of grace" for the saloon is a disgrace.

A boozer is the one-legged man in the race of life.

A whiskey blossom on your nose blooms the year 'round.

An overdrawn nature account and bank account spell failure.

The race today is not for the swiftest but for the soberest.

Putting alcohol in your system is like throwing gasoline on a flame.

A saloon sign, "Workingmen's Home," should be "Workingmen's Morgue."

The public school is the foundation of life; the public saloon is the foundation of death.

A man can go through mercantile bankruptcy several times—booze bankruptcy but once.

FRANCISGRAMS

Think before you drink.

An eye opener closes the eyes.

The men who booze are the men who lose.

The best substitute for the saloon is the home.

Booze ruins one internally, externally and eternally.

Americans must kill King Alcohol, or he will kill them.

Watch your step—that it doesn't lead you into the saloons.

It's a short road from good fellowship to good for nothingness.

The monarchy of King Alcohol seems to be turning into a dry republic.

Public opinion supressed firecrackers, and public opinion will supress fire water.

If George Washington could come back to America today, he would write another farewell letter—and die.

You can't get a man to eat honey that contains a live bee—but you can get a man to drink whiskey that contains a live snake.

JUST A WORD PERSONAL

A CHICAGO business man, known the country over as a humanitarian; a liberal and charitable gentleman; one of the most successful in his chosen work in the United States, asked permission to read the manuscript of "My Last Drink." Here is his written opinion:

ALDERMAN, I have read your experience with the demon and how you conquered him. Publish it so that every man and woman in the country may read it. Send your story out into the world as a warning. If men will read your story, and re-read it, until it is written on their memories you will have done a greater service for humanity than any man of the present generation; more for mankind than any agency or any thousand men have done in many, many years. Give it, Alderman, every word of your history and experience. Every employer in the country should place a copy of "My Last Drink" in the hands of every man in his employ.

AND SO IT IS PRINTED!

Only when facts and expositions about drink are given to the public by a human living being—one who has traveled the terrible alcoholic road to ruin—do they have reality, color, warmth, or convincing power.

CHAPTER ONE

My First Drink and My Fall

HENRY WARD BEECHER once said:
"The man who is worth while is the one who bares his life and experience for the benefit of his fellow men."

A man who played both ends of the game of life certainly possesses qualifications as a judge. For years I occupied a front seat on the infernal brink of drink.

I spare myself nothing in this tragic recital. It is not made in a boastful manner, but in a heart full of humiliation and had it another object but warning to my fellow men, would shame a man to his grave.

9

Degraded? Yes. This is a story of degradation. Hence, I am only outlining, hinting, whispering, hoping that some poor human being may be warned and saved from starting on a campaign of drink that will end in wreck——wreck of everything that is kind, sensitive, human and honorable.

I had the honor of enumerating among my friends, Governor Edward F. Dunne, and Charles S. Deneen of Illinois, Mayors William Hale Thompson, Carter H. Harrison, Fred A. Busse, and nearly all of the leading judges in the Circuit, Superior and Municipal Courts of Chicago; many of the leading bankers and business men of Chicago and in hundreds of cities throughout the United States. With all these associations, and connections and surroundings that any man should be proud of, I tottered and fell——a hopeless victim of drink.

I had more opportunities than the average man. I was successful in business, had the dis-

A whiskey drinker never dies——he is dead before the start.
Thinkers are not drinkers.

MY LAST DRINK

tinction of being a Chicago Alderman, was honored with other public offices, was a delegate to a political National Convention. I had wealth, excellent health and most substantial prosperity. I had a business that paid me annually a good many thousands of dollars, had a beautiful home in one of Chicago's most aristocratic districts, had automobiles, servants, and all the good things of life that go with sobriety, wealth, refinement, ambition, and respect; a member and officer in a number of Chicago's leading social and commercial clubs, a Thirty-second Degree Mason, a publisher and owner of one of America's largest magazines; the author of several standard works, a happy family and devoted wife—all swallowed up in the whirlpool of drink. I drank up my prospects and fortune; I drank up my friendships, and there were never more devoted and long suffering friends. I drank up a home—the home of my wife and family—and saw them turned penniless into the street.

A saloon thrives on widows' tears, mother's heartaches and starving children.

MY LAST DRINK

And with that sight in my mind I still drank harder and harder, brooding over the troubles I had created for myself, getting deeper in the meshes of the snake day by day. No argument, restraint, or treatment, could stay my insatiable thirst and desire for drink—it seemed as though only death could win the battle for me.

Drink held me in bondage. I was not my own master. I was a helpless victim, being held with a strangle hold. Try as I would, I could not escape from the demon alcohol. He pursued me everywhere. From coast to coast and across the ocean, he was my constant companion. I was bound, brain, hand and foot. How should I break this terrible chain binding me to this chariot of destruction?

Heart and head refused to receive the terrible warning handed to me in tremors, sickness and loss of health and all worldly possessions—until at last whiskey won its fell victory, and I was whipped, ruined and disgraced.

A boozer may fool himself, but he cannot fool nature.
A whiskey smile soon turns to a frown.

MY LAST DRINK

Like thousands of drinkers, I banked on my superior will power and resistance to prevent me from falling to the bottom. But the snake-hole was open and down, down to the bottom I dropped, forced into poverty, crime and prison. I partook freely of the juice proffered by the serpent and was stung, stung nearly to death. I sank to the level and class of a tramp. Booze had done its work, and left me a mental wreck.

I used to reason that the other fellow was drinking too much for his own good and should let up. I was positive I was all right and could quit drinking anytime I wanted to. But when I tried to do so I made an inglorious failure.

I am not posing as a horrible example, but as a living example of what can be accomplished when a man just resolves to quit the habit. Neither am I a reformer, but rather an informer to those that are following the path I did, to inform them that the same abyss of disaster is awaiting to consume them unless they clamp

A corkscrew is straight compared with the average saloon keeper.

the lid on drink quickly and permanently. And I want to warn every drinking man—a moderate, occasional or periodical drinker who reads these lines—the chances are 100 to 1 that if you don't quit the game you will wake up some day and find yourself at the tail end of the procession, the same as I did. You may be a man of delicate sensibility, of lofty purpose, and of towering intellect; you may have qualities which, untainted by alcohol, would adorn any character, but if addicted to whiskey, your destruction is certain.

When did this work of ruin begin?

I acquired the drinking habit just the same as thousands of others have and are acquiring it today. I drank whiskey just as myriads of men do; drank and thought I attended to business, prospered for a time, kept my health and head for a time, provided for my family, was a "good fellow," and easily maintained my position in the community. I was forming an awful habit.

The best substitute for the saloon is the home.
Moderation in drinking is damnation in embryo.

I was slipping every day. I didn't realize it. My friends did.

My first step in drink was in the very best drinking places, where I met and drank daily with well-groomed, high-class, respectable gentlemen. With these "good" companions I contracted uncontrollable habits which led me to the brink. When a shabbily dressed man would enter a bar room, one whom I had known in former years as a successful man, one of my associates would say:

"There's Bill Smith. Five years ago he was a successful broker in LaSalle Street. Old booze has him by the neck."

We passed it off with a laugh and another drink, feeling cocksure we would never get in the condition of Bill Smith. Oh, no! But nearly every one of us got there.

I used to take a drink at the club, at social gatherings, at political blowouts, weddings, etc., and all places where the alleged spirit of good fellowship presented itself. I would never turn

A lazy man never kicks when carrying a heavy load of booze.
An eye opener closes the eyes.

my glass down when the champagne, wine and booze came along. Always had it right side up for another helping. I thought I was having a good time. Here is where I fooled myself as all men do who are drinking—just for company's sake.

My descent was slow at first, but as the appetite grew I dropped from the moderate class to the rapid and confirmed ranks.

As it was noised among my friends that I was drinking too much, getting to be a drunkard in fact, at first my self respect was shocked and I felt as though I could not again face my friends and the world with the same high consciousness of worth and manhood as before. I had been called a drunkard. I began to believe it. One feels that he is in imminent danger of becoming the worst of outcasts, a confirmed drunkard, a burden and disgrace to his friends and community. The physical suffering which he endures is nothing to his mental torture. It seems to him as though

Whiskey is the monkey wrench in the machinery of efficiency.

every person whom he meets is aware of his feelings and disgrace, and look upon him as a ruined, drunken, degraded man. His resolutions of reformation are usually like ropes of sand. Mine were; I was powerless to throw the dragon off.

I had aspirations, ambitions, successes, and wealth; my shambling figure once walked as proudly as any man; a real man in a world of men. I strangled those thoughts, in more drink, that I might not be tortured any more. My passion for drink brought additional darkness, and desolation. Home, family, business and friends, swallowed in the maelstrom of drink. As I would walk the street I could see old friends pointing me out and discussing my condition.

Knowing all these things but too fully steeped in drink to realize, I kept plunging forward. The demon seemed to have put a death hold on me. Try as I would there did not seem to be any avenue of escape.

Drinking men are the architects of their own misfortunes. What is a chaser? Ask the snake in the whiskey.

MY LAST DRINK

Often a friend would place his hand on my shoulder and say, "Alderman, you are hitting your brain against a bottle a little too often, your face shows it, your actions and condition show it. Better put the brakes on or you will meet with an awful collision one of these days."

I felt somewhat peeved at this advice, feeling like all drinking men, that it was nobody's business but my own; that I was all right and could quit anytime I wished. I didn't quit, I couldn't quit. I was anchored soul, body and mind to the monster.

I tried and struggled and resolved many times to drink no more. But the beast was only scotched, not caged. My strength and will power to resist was dead.

Every mental faculty was unhinged and every physical power benumbed and my whole being was rendered helpless and degraded, and in this condition I committed crimes and acts that no sane man would ever dream of.

The saloons do not need regulation, they need strangulation.
Booze boycotts the brain.

MY LAST DRINK

Drink first destroys or injures what is most sensitive, most important, the brain. No man who has hls system polluted with whiskey can be depended upon for anything, and you cannot trust yourself, you are drunk at the top, for every drop of alcohol goes there first. Your mind and brain are clouded by alcoholic paralysis. From the top down—that is the way whiskey works on a man; it ruins first what is highest in him— the moral qualities so carefully acquired in the long years of evolution. It is the most fragile part of the mental machinery that is first impaired —that which has been recently and most carefully built up in the creation of character—the moral part.

A man is a fool who requires to be taught by bitter experience that alcohol is a monster that will destroy. So don't experiment with it—take a victim's word that it is fatal to tempt or trifle with.

At last whiskey had done its cruel work. I

Columbus discovered America, John Barleycorn, Personal Liberty.

MY LAST DRINK

became a confirmed, drunken wretch, forsaken, it seemed, by God and man, pitied by some, despised by others, a burden and disgrace to my family and friends and the community. I finally became a wandering outcast in the world, experiencing the awful happenings that are the life of a helpless, hopeless drunkard.

CHAPTER TWO

Dark Side of a Drinking Man's Life

M Y PASSION for drink continued to grow and darkness and desolation met me at every turn.

Imagining myself a strong willed man I did not think of the possibility of defeat from drink. I was aware that whiskey had ruined my home and prospects and blighted many a brilliant brain. I was not as strong mentally as I figured. This was the weakness of my equipment for the fight. I didn't know it then but as I kept drifting down the valley of gloom and despair I then realized the sadness of my condition.

An old man of 60 with white hair is today more in demand than a young man of 30 with a red nose.

MY LAST DRINK

The hospitals and poor houses and jails are full of men who imagined they had strong minds and argued to themselves they could quit any time. Booze is a sure loser for any man. I used to be one of the wise ones who would say, "I can quit it any time I want to." That's a joke. About the time you think you want to quit you are about three-quarters of the way to being a drunkard or bum, and something seems to say, "What's the use of stopping, might as well finish the course," and your finish is always a bad one, too. Your appetite is increasing, drink is gaining on you, and gains with every man who tampers with it.

When a man allows his alcoholic appetite to control him, he is turning his body into a charnel house, and is slowly but surely approaching an awful chasm of distress, and digging his own pathway down to hell.

No man ever made the desperate struggle that I did. The attitude of the world was cruel at times. I figured it was a battle no man could

It is just a short crooked road from moderate drinking to drunkenness.

win and that thousands have lost. The liquid devil seemed to be unconquerable. I would fight and resolve and fall and go down to defeat. I had learned at an awful cost the terrible power of whiskey.

My friends used to say to me, "Why don't you cut it out, Alderman?" I was powerless, the habit had enslaved me. If you saw a soldier with a sword thrust through his body, pinioning him to a tree would these same people say to him, "Why don't you pull it out? Why don't you be free?"

This battle to be free from the curse of drink is a long, cruel and silent one and you must do your fighting alone, too.

One bitter cold morning I stood in front of the Auditorium Hotel, watching well-dressed, properly nourished, prosperous men leaving for their offices, many of whom were my associates and friends in my sober, prosperous days. When I saw these men, for a moment the fact came to my

Putting alcohol in your system is like throwing gasoline on a flame.

mind that I once was like them and I had aspirations and successes, and ambitions that soared as high as the morning star, and I broke and bruised and strangled their beautiful wings under the blighting curse of drink.

Birth, wealth, power, education and genius all fall before this horrible vice—drink.   No one is immune who drinks; age is no barrier.

I was maudlin and nervous from drink; hungry, and my clothes spotted and frazzled. The sight of these gentlemen filled me with bitter memories and remorse.   I was still drifting towards the goal of destruction.

And there I stood, a homeless, friendless tramp, a man in whom every good impulse was dead.   All, all swallowed in the whirlpool of drink, a shambling, wobbly, drunken outcast.   I was a pitiable spectacle.

I had slept the night before on the cold, cement floor of the Harrison Street police station. I slept as a tired dog sleeps, a dog worn out with

A reputation for sobriety is today a letter of credit.
A little drink makes a big man shrink.

a fruitless chase, and laid there drunk as one dead on the icy, hard floor. My companions were the same I met at all police stations throughout the country, tramps, burglars, pickpockets and the usual class picked up by the city police and "thrown in" for the night. With the same moan nearly all assigned drink as the contributing cause of their downfall.

Where could I go? What could I do? There was no friendly hand or cheering word for me any more. I had betrayed and saddened all my old friends and acquaintances. The first thought always of a discouraged drinking man is more drink. For a time whiskey fades your trouble, temporarily your bitter thoughts are hushed, and drowsy forgetfulness pervades your brain and your terrible condition is forgotten in stupefaction.

I shuffled into a saloon on State street, grabbed a few mouthfuls of free lunch, staggered to a chair and in a few minutes was dead in sleep.

If you want to pluck the flower of sorrow follow the booze route.

MY LAST DRINK

Horrible dreams troubled and harassed me.
After about thirty minutes of this torture, a strong
hand had me by the shoulder and out into the
street the "good" saloon keeper threw me, minus
my hat, which a "guest" had relieved me of
while I slept.

I was in a state of awful, cruel depression.
I felt as though the weight of the world was upon
me and bearing me down, down. I wanted something to lift this weight. I didn't know what it
was. I took a jolt of whiskey, but it had little or
no effect on me unless it was to make me feel more
miserable. Upon my head and heart and brow
was the remorseless iron cross of suffering. Like
a treacherous and underhanded foe alcohol sat
enthroned.

You can see what an awful battle for life
confronts a whiskey slave. Whiskey is a demon
put on earth by the devil to torture the souls of
men.

There is something unnatural about the

It's a short road from good-fellowship to good-for-
nothingness.

26

person who can look upon human sorrow, without being himself affected. Even in my helpless condition I did what little I could to assist many unfortunates, although I was as bad off as they were.

I drifted into a low groggery on North Clark street, Chicago, when in walked a bleared eyed, unshaven man about fifty years of age, clothed in rags and dirt. With trembling hands and voice he said:

"Pard, slip me a jitney for a brain duster. I must have a drink or I will die." I gave the unfortunate man a nickel. I was interested in him. One could see he had been a man in his day, and after his drink he was quite voluble. I pried into his past.

He eyed me with a pathetic look and arising from a beer keg on which he was seated he was indeed a study.

And there he stood with a grace and dignity that all his rags and dirt could not obscure, and without any prelude he said:

Let us crush these booze artists in human slaughter.
Booze ruins one internally, externally and eternally.

MY LAST DRINK

"I am a graduate of Yale. Ever hear of Yale? Splendid educational institution. You'd never believe it if I told you," he drawled. "Some of the old men around Chicago remember me. I was a criminal lawyer." He whispered his name, which was a truly honorable one until drink gripped him. "Ten years ago seems a long time, but it wasn't so long in the going. Started boozing accidentally. Took a sniff of it at the club or a social function. I did it, though I knew it was wrong, and have been doing it ever since. To-day I am a human wreck, my end is near."

He plucked nervously at his coat, straightened his tie, brushed his hand across his face and in a sorrowing voice slowly said: "Awful nervous. Stuff makes you nervous. Leaps through your brain. Sets it afire." And he fell over in a whiskey fit on the floor. A policeman was called; the "wagon" came rumbling up and he was carted to the East Chicago Avenue police station, and upon arriving there was dead. It was a sad death.

Watch your step—that it doesn't lead you into the saloons. The men who booze are the men who lose.

MY LAST DRINK

There was no comfort on that dying pillow. No sweet repose. The gentle hand of mother, wife, or daughter was missing. No voice of consolation or friendship. Dying alone and like a dog.

There is a sermon in this man's life, Mr. Drinker!

Notwithstanding this terrible lesson I continued to drink and drift. My companions were that great army of whiskey soaked wretches, thousands of whom had been respectable and honored men until booze seduced them, always circulating between the barrel houses, cheap lodging houses, saloons, police stations, jails, hospitals and poor house.

There was nothing too dangerous for me to attempt to secure money to appease my burning and horrible thirst for whiskey. I must have drink. Wandering from city to city, state to state, I was insane and aimless in my thoughts, stupid and benumbed from drink and kept on wandering, wandering, and drinking, drinking. A period in

A saloon keeper's friendship is tied with a rope of sand.
Think before you drink.

MY LAST DRINK

jail in Richmond, Va., Portland, Maine, or San Diego, Cal., or of any other twenty-five cities I could name, had no deterring effect. I would make resolutions, however, but I was chained to the brute and it seemed as though no human effort could break the fetters.

The mind of a strong man soon becomes palsied from drink. His brain weakens, his character falls, his judgment is worthless and his life useless, and any man that drinks is certainly taking a long chance on being trapped.

It seems unbelievable, this hideous thing which had happened to me. I slowly recalled the steps by which I had arrived at this disaster. I was not so far gone but what I could remember some things, but past performances did not appeal to me. Nothing appealed to me but drink.

I soon discovered that it was not the barrel houses, cheap saloons and groggeries and slums and rookeries of alcoholism that do the worst work. These places are only way stations on the

A glass of booze is a ticket in the lottery of death.
Good intentions never enter saloon doors.

road to death. Where did that bloated, ulcerous, wheezing wretch that comes hobbling and staggering out of a barrel house, get his habit started? Certainly not in a barrel house, but at one of the so-called respectable saloons, restaurants, clubs or the bar of a leading hotel.

"Is a man insane when he is drinking?" Yes, and it is a strange and weird insanity. When I was drinking I knew I was myself, but had no power to be myself. This appears paradoxical but it is true. I was occasionally rational and lucid in act and speech, but it was not the rationality and lucidity of my real self, it was always the conduct of a personality the opposite to my own.

Whiskey is a murderer, and the law should treat it as a deadly poison, and treat those who make it and sell it, after the passage of suitable laws, as they would treat any other dealer in a poisonous, murderous agency. In every foot of the United States territory whiskey should be

The only man in the universe that can get full and keep his head with him is the man in the moon.

declared by federal law, by state law and by declaration of the interstate commerce authorities a poison, and its sale a crime.

My saddest experiences in grappling with drink were yet to come.

CHAPTER THREE

Why Men Drink

DRINKING baffles us, confounds us, shames us and mocks us at every point. It outwits the man of business and the worker.

Why men drink? Any man that drinks can assign many reasons, not one of which is logical or tenable. I have known thousands of really good men who, discouraged and badgered, and pressed in their business have taken away the keen vitality of their life by resorting to the cup and this habit thus formed finally led to their downfall. Is not this going on all the time? Are there not hundreds and thousands of cases, almost

---

Which will you choose—the Field of Honor or the Potter's Field.

---

in our very midst, of persons who have in some such way become victims of this terrible scourge? No sane man should drink to drown trouble. It cannot be done. You are simply chaining failure to your life. I did. I discovered that a clear brain and sober body will overcome trouble quicker than booze. In some cases whiskey creates an increased brilliancy at first, but it is a temporary and suicidal flash only, burning out swiftly into the ashes of an utter ruin. I need not repeat to any reader the names of men, once renowned for intellectual attainments, but afterward degraded by strong drink to the stupidity and loathsomeness of a sot.

Never delude yourself that you need a bracer. The use of a bracer is dead wrong. Bracers destroy the warning signals of nature to tired, exhausted men. Bracers abolish fatigue for the moment, but fatigue warns the body that rest and recreation are necessary. This bracing drink is ofttimes the beginning of an awful end. I

A man can go through mercantile bankruptcy several times —booze bankruptcy but once.

know that whiskey poisons and shortens life. Whiskey does not give strength. I was deluded into that belief to my awful sorrow. I felt stronger for the moment after taking a drink but it was simply temporary delusion. I had irritation, and aggravation, not strength, and I was unwittingly consuming one day the capital for the next. I was running in debt to nature.

It is a foolish sociability, the desire for showing friendship and being agreeable that influences many men to drink whiskey. It is not for any good it is going to do them or any particular happiness that it affords, but it is this sociability. Man is a sociable being and he looks for some fellow man in discussing questions of the day, his troubles, and things of that sort, but he can cultivate a taste for something besides whiskey—something that will not enslave and ruin.

As a rule a man drinks to excess with a definite end in view—principally that he may acquire power to be something more than he naturally is.

A saloon keeper floats the American flag and hands you a shroud.

MY LAST DRINK

He is depressed, and he wants to be cheerful; he is timid and he desires to be brave; he is going to "touch" someone and needs a little more steam and nerve; he is cold and wishes to be warm; he is feeble in mind and body and wants the world to look brighter—and quickly, too.

One of the many reasons men cling to alcoholic drinks is the belief in their value for nourishment and strength. The moment these idols fall to the ground the better for them. Public schools should universally teach upon this most important subject.

How can whiskey drown trouble when it will not drown a snake?

Mental depression and nervousness caused by overwork drives many men to try whiskey. The higher the nervous strain, once the habit is formed, the more whiskey is needed and demanded. You are then in the drunkard class, but don't realize it. You don't believe it; I didn't either. But when I made up my mind to quit I

Battling with booze is like trying to corner the wind.
A saloon keeper is simply a stoker for the devil.

didn't have any mind, no will power, no power of resistance. I was gone. A little rest, recreation, or sleep is better than all the stimulant in the world for a man who feels run down. This imaginary physical condition has started thousands of men on the road to ruin. Once you fool with drink you are liable to find the habit fixed before you are aware of it.

Thousands of men drink for an imaginary weakness of the stomach, and a faintness and goneness, especially when they arise in the morning. Others imagine whiskey aids digestion, when as a matter of fact it retards it. But the most nonsensical habit of all is the poisonous "night cap" before retiring. Never take this night drink to aid tired nerves and produce sleep, which is a cruel fallacy.

The solid mass of men who make up the aristocratic clubs of all cities never drink to get drunk but I have seen thousands of them land in the "has-been" class. Such men work at

The race today is not for the swiftest but for the soberest.
Safety first means sober first.

high pressure, hard and fast in business hours; and they continue to drink in order to work harder, always feeling that they are too wise and strong headed to become a victim of drink, but some day they fall, and I found all cities full of broken down club men and "brilliants," and professional men, acting as night cashiers in lunch rooms, watchmen, doortenders, and other light positions, and always bent on telling you who they know and of their former greatness. The only man they knew real well was John Barleycorn.

Any man who attempts to "drown his sorrows in the flowing bowl" is doomed from the start.

When a man first starts out to be a "regular fellow," and has money and health and position, a little stimulant gives him a fictitious value of his greatness and importance. He is charmed and delighted when he plunges into a grandly equipped, gorgeous and well-lighted saloon. He is pleased with the pleasant smile and welcome of the proprietor. The handy third rail for your

The public school is the foundation of life; the public saloon is the foundation of death.

foot, the mahogany bar for your service and the alleged hearty good fellowship surroundings drive away all care and thought of the morrow, all of which is the first degree in the drama of destruction.

A little whiskey with your friends at this time and place, you reason, is not so bad. As time goes on you require more drink, the habit is forming and finally, taking too much of the poison, you are not wanted in one of the fine drinking places,—the barrel house for yours.

Come back to the smiling bartender when you are broke, unshaven and unkempt, and ask for a drink, "just for old time's sake." That smile has turned to a frown and a refusal. The saloonkeeper is smiling and breaking in a new batch of victims. All drinking men finally go the same route and land at the same station—Death.

I have been in splendid whiskey places, with liveried bartenders, masterpieces of painting on the wall, furnishings, rugs, and divans, and loung-

It is only a short life from the Blackstone to the Bridewell. Whiskey is not included in the scheme of life.

ing chairs not equalled in a Turkish harem, where you could loll and loaf and fill your hide with poison. The grandeur of the surroundings dignifies you while the whiskey stupefies you. This life is a short and merry one and lack of money pushes you down the scale. I have drunk champagne in the Blackstone, squirrel booze in a barrel house and finally wound up on soup in the Bridewell. Which do you suppose I enjoyed the most?

Drunkenness is certainly the most peculiar of all vices. A man can gamble and still make money. He can live an unmoral life and do the same; but if he is habitually intoxicated he loses the power of self-support, and, of course, the power of providing for his family. This is the reason why society interferes, and has the right to interfere, with the custom of drinking. The drink evil is a handicap for any race to carry, just as tuberculosis or yellow fever are handicaps. It impairs vitality, reduces efficiency, energy,

There are sixty different kinds of religious creeds in the United States, but only one kind of saloon.

initiative and working power. Any man who tries to cheat himself in playing the game of life will always find conditions stacked against him. Whiskey disappoints and betrays all but those who deliberately seek death for body and mind.

Alcohol is the drunkard's hangman, its aid is treacherous, it betrays and depraves him. He struts for a while and glorifies himself on whiskey's prowess which he arrogates as his own; but his self deception is patent, and is presently exposed. In short, excitement from drink imposes upon a man a selfhood which is not his own, but a false and monstrous exaggeration of it. At first it seems to give him strength of faculty beyond his normal, but rapidly it hurries him into folly and danger and ends by sousing him ignobly and helplessly in the gutter.

The similarity of drunkenness to insanity or madness has always been noticed; it dilates a good man into a monster—and then an alcoholic imbecile. Men filled with liquor have been known

Booze is the misery of many for the gain of a few.
A whiskey blossom on your nose blooms the year 'round.

to commit all the crimes in the calendar without being properly conscious of the fact. Insanity could do no more.

Treating is another bad feature of the drinking habit. If you met a friend in a grocery store and he purchased a pound of sugar he would not ask you to step up and have a pound. If you are in a saloon and the same friend comes in to buy a drink he will ask you to have something with him. If treating were abolished in the United States it would be a step in the right direction. That is to say, when a person wishes to take a drink of intoxicating liquor he may not invite a friend to drink with him. Thousands of men would be unable to secure a drink if it were not for some acquaintance treating them. I have been broke for weeks, in every section of the United States, but drinks were always plenty, through treating.

In the United States one or two commonwealths that have not banished the saloon have

A street car says:—"Pay as you enter." A saloon, "Die as you enter."

sought to destroy the treating habit by passing laws against it. But it seems to be difficult to uphold enactments of that sort.

The bane of all drink holes is this miserable custom—the saloon etiquette of treating. "I'm just going to take a drink, won't you join me?" This game is fostered and systematically nursed by all saloon keepers in the so-called respectable saloon as well as the lowest groggery—and every drinking man knows what I say is true. Saloon treating is a wicked and pernicious habit and should be blotted out of every community.

A strict and enforced anti-treating law would cause thousands of saloons to cease business.

CHAPTER FOUR

The Moderate Drinker

MODERATE drinking is the father of all drunkenness. All experience declares its truth. The moderate consumers of intoxicating drinks are the chief agents in promoting and perpetuating drunkenness. Moderate drinking is the beginning of that inclined plane which will slide you easily to destruction. It seems pleasant and safe at first, but the end will be demoralizing. Take a former moderate drinking victim's word for that.

The moderate drinker is the great stumbling block to sobriety. It is not the drunkard in the gutter that a young man has in his mind when he

---

Americans must kill King Alcohol, or he will kill them.
Booze is the best stranger in the world.

---

takes his first drink. It is his respectable moderate drinking neighbor. He reasons what harm can there be in drinking when such men drink booze and beer at high class bars and clubs and even under their own roof. The higher a man stands in a community the greater is his influence either for good or evil.

There are thousands upon thousands who are weak, of excitable temperament, easily tempted, strong passioned, and to whom moderation in the use of alcoholic stimulant as a beverage almost inevitably lead to dissipation and ruin.

Intemperance is supported and perpetuated by the moderate drinker. The moderate drinker of to-day is the outcast of the next decade. That continued tippling will create an appetite and a mastery that no man can easily shake off.

Ask any man who has been a slave to drink where the evil first began. He will tell you, of course, in his first glass. Always in the moderate use of it. Didn't take much at first, didn't care

A saloon sign, "Workingmen's Home," should be "Workingmen's Morgue."

anything about it. Could stop it any time he wished. Always boasting of his vain confidence of being able to control his appetite and to stop just at the proper time. But in the booze there was an adder, unseen and shifty, that stung the moderate drinker, that forced him into unwilling excesses. Any man that trifles with booze is liable to be stung to death as it has stung millions.

The victims from moderate drinkers are selected from the most promising, generous, social, and affectionate of our business men. Genius, education, family, profession, friends, furnish no abiding obstacle or sure defense. When the degrading appetite has been formed and whetted, it bursts through all these bonds. The noblest and most cherished sons of our best connections are here cast to perish with the vilest and the basest of mankind.

I have met socalled high-class men at the most pretentious drinking places in all parts of the country licking up the poison "only in modera-

Public opinion suppressed firecrackers, and public opinion will suppress fire water.

46

tion." Hundreds of these men are models of morality, respectability, and piety in the world of business. They know the tendency of appetite. Know how the love for strong drink usually increases until the moderate sip becomes a regular beverage and the small glass is exchanged for a larger one until the taste becomes a fixed habit and the moderate drinker is transformed into a toper, and the toper into a drunken sot.

So-called respectable moderate drinkers who drink at the onyx bars do not believe that any considerable number of men who are drunk are served with drinks in saloons. In the high-class, expensively equipped cafes, and saloons, sober bartenders, sober cashiers, sober managers, and sober porters usually refuse to serve drinks to drunks or to poorly dressed, down-and-out appearing persons; they want the money just the same, but some high browed, moderate drinker, who is a good spender would object to their company. If you are well groomed you can go to the best

If George Washington could come back to America today he would write another farewell letter—and die.

MY LAST DRINK

bar in the world and if your looks, speech or action indicate you have been drinking, that's no hindrance, if you've got the coin. But in alleged respectable saloons, noisy souses, sleepers, loungers, or pan-handlers are not allowed to hang around unless they are known to the management. The jails, bridewells, houses of correction, penitentiaries, state prisons, pens, asylums, hospitals, and reformatories have many guests to-day that a few years back were hail fellows well met, just moderate drinkers, at the leading bars, cafes, clubs, and hotels — pitiful, dying, miserable wretches.

I met in New Orleans, La., a man well-known throughout the south, a former banker with unlimited wealth, and powerful business connections, broken in health and fortune and a social outcast. He was a complete alcoholic wreck. Every one who had known him in his successful days avoided and shunned him. I met him in a cheap saloon, begging and crying for "just one more drink."

Champagne bottle to black bottle is within easy reach.
A saloon is the hell gate on the road to success.

MY LAST DRINK

I was interested in the man after learning of his former standing in the community. He told me he started in as a moderate drinker, just one or two drinks a day. The habit almost unconsciously grew on him. Slight business reverses came. Instead of battling them with a clear head he took more drink. In a trembling voice and a staggering gait, bent and decrepit, he walked to a chair and with effort seating himself, said:

"Ten years ago I was just a moderate drinker. But that habit caused my downfall. When I had my first run of hard luck," he said, "I turned to whiskey. I wanted to feel good again. Whiskey does it for a while. It makes you feel that you're a fine fellow and that you'd be a millionaire if you could only get what was coming to you. What a warning my condition ought to be to my whiskey drinking acquaintances. Whiskey made me forget my troubles, but it also made me forget my ambitions. It was my undoing. Whiskey has robbed me of home, family, wealth, health, posi-

Some men's idea of pleasure is to do things that bring them misery.

tion, character, business, friends, self respect, and everything but life itself. It makes the world look brighter for a little while. When I started to climb up again I found that I had lost my punch. That made me feel bad, and I went back to whiskey to feel good again."

"And there you are!" he said, "Down and out."

"Why don't you quit?" I asked.

"Forget it; you can't quit when you get where I am," and with a pitying look and as plaintive voice as man ever heard, he slowly continued; "I am waiting to reach one more bar, where I will not plead for drink but mercy. I know my end is near."

And if Mr. Moderate Drinker doesn't take a quick inventory of the condition he is drifting to it will not be many years before he will be unable to stem the tide that is bound to overwhelm him.

When the testing time comes the moderate drinker is always found wanting. The drink habit

The evil that saloon keepers do lives after them.
A boozer has a dent in his brain.

has grown unconsciously upon him. He hesitates resolves, and then falls. He is now in the second degree of a drunkard's life. He is easily and quickly initiated in the third and final degree, a lost man.

There is no such other one source of woe and crime in the world as the excessive indulgence in alcoholic drink. And the excess of indulgence comes in a vast majority of cases from drinking in moderation. There is that in the very nature of alcohol that tends to excite thirst for deeper draughts of it. If we stop the moderation, we are sure of arresting a large amount of the excess.

Now that business men of the country—cold-blooded, unsentimental, mathematical, rigidly scientific—have stepped in and told their employees that drinking men are not wanted, the moderate, occasional, periodical and habitual drinker is waking up and taking notice. The Illinois Steel Company in South Chicago have erected an immense electric sign over the entrance to their

Don't go to the capitals of Europe to see old ruins. Just take a walk through the streets of any American city.

works reading: "Did Booze Ever Do You Any Good?"

Of course those who have followed medical and scientific progress during the past few years and those who have interested themselves in the new science of human efficiency, know why big business, railroad and commercial organizations are taking this stand. But does it not seem strange that these marchers behind the booze banner should so willfully close their eyes to the changed attitude of nearly all employers of help, the men who heretofore have commanded their willing subservience!

Can't they see that nearly all business houses already have broken with booze? The man who drinks is putting a burdensome mortgage on his future. Business don't want him, society won't have him and his end is not difficult to predict.

The drinking man, moderate or otherwise, nowadays, soon finds his credit gone, efficiency and economy spoiled, ability and industry squandered,

---

The monarchy of King Alcohol seems to be turning into a dry republic.

---

honesty impaired and confidence of friends forfeited. They soon become fit only for the most menial positions in life.

Whiskey cheats and marches under false colors. It attacks the old and the young, and knows no rules of warfare. I want to tell the young man who thinks he can "take whiskey or leave it alone" or drink in moderation, that what he says is perfectly true. He can take it or leave it alone. But if he takes it he will probably find that the time will come he can't leave it alone. I found this to be true in my case.

A man that drinks is always behind in the procession of life. He is carrying too heavy a handicap.

Nature is the great law maker and it does not require a detective to find the man who violates her laws. The world is what it is and he who disdains to pursue the sober, honest paths that lead to worldly success and honor, is dedicated to poverty and disgrace.

Decoration Day for old soldiers, Desecration Day for old soaks.

MY LAST DRINK

Could the man who today is only a moderate drinker, be induced to take an inventory of himself and look carefully into my experience and be made to understand what a dreary thing it is when a man shall feel himself going down a precipice with open eyes and a passive will—to see his destruction and have no will power to stop it, and yet to know he is himself to blame, to know that all goodness has left him, and yet not to be able to forget a time when it was otherwise—just brooding over the piteous spectacle of his own self ruin, I believe he would stop his half formed habit at once.

The history of alcoholism presents a tragedy, the first act begins with a moderate use of the poison and the second and last act finds you a complete victim, and if you escape living a life of drunkenness, vagabondism and crime you are indeed lucky.

CHAPTER FIVE

Experience With Saloons and Saloon Keepers

DON'T forget, young man, that when you enter a drinking place and the saloon keeper smiles and welcomes you and gives you a hearty handshake, that the claw of the tiger can always be felt in the grip.

In a wide and variegated experience in saloons, reaching from ocean to ocean, and from Canada to Mexico, a fact that stands out most prominently with me is the sameness of men and ideas of saloon keepers, a hard, listless, unfeeling lot, that once in a while perform some little act of generosity, like giving you a drink or car

---

You don't find comfort or prosperity in the home of a booze fighter.

55

fare, and then imagine they are generous and good fellows. That's all it is—imagination.

There is plenty of artificial good fellowship in a saloon keeper when a man spends money or a live one drops in. I recollect a Chicago physician spending a Hundred and Fifty Dollars at a Dearborn street bar one night and heard the saloon keeper in a gruff and villainous manner refuse him a drink next morning when he was suffering for it.

The men that own gin mills are different from grocers and other tradesmen around them. They are a harder, tougher, low-browed type, singularly impervious to human sympathy or interest in any matter whatever except the coin and the music of the ring of the cash register, which seems to soothe their robbing breasts. Even when pleasant young fellows go into this business they lapse into the "gin-head" type in a short time. Two well-known young men, semi-professional athletes, popular, jolly, healthy

When you see a prominent citizen trying to unlock his front door with a lead pencil, look out.

home boys, went into the saloon business in the loop district in Chicago, but today both are typical saloon keepers, hard, sneering, and broken in health.

There is a reason for all this. One sees a lot of human nature in all lines of business. The saloon keeper sees more and more of it than anybody else. Everybody is trying to stick the saloon keeper. If he passes you too much change one never hands it back, for every regular patron of a saloon knows he is bunked on drinks and short changed at any and all times it is convenient.

The saloon is referred to by many as the "Poor Man's Club." Well, it is rightly named, it is clubbing the brains out of many a poor devil. Others are labeled "Workingmen's Home." This is a misnomer. It should read:—"Workingmen's Morgue."

A poor man's club! Isn't that rich? No dues, no passwords, you are known by signs. A red

A saloon keeper's cash register bell is the devil's chime.
Gin and genius make a faulty team.

nose and ragged clothes and almost shoeless feet proves you are a life member. You pay no more dues, only to nature. And when you shuffle off, who buries you and looks after your family? The saloon keeper? Oh, no! It is your sober, law abiding neighbors of course, and the general public is taxed for their maintenance.

You will hear defenders of the liquor traffic make the statement that saloon keepers are "good fellows." If you think a saloon keeper is a good fellow, call on one you have spent all your money with and ask him for a drink. When an old timer comes in, a miserable, trembling tramp, and begs for a drink, he will be refused and ordered out of the saloon. That tramp may be you a few years from now—you, man, that can drink or let it alone.

How many, many times have I heard men remark, "Where can a poor down and out go for a bite and rest but a saloon?"

When you are hungry, broke and almost

A home is a vested right; a saloon a vested wrong.
Whiskey is the devil in liquid form.

perishing for a drink, did you ever go into a saloon for relief? I have, a thousand times, in saloons in every city in the United States. And such a hearty reception you receive.

Walk into a saloon for a free lunch, broke. You step up to the slop-jar of soup and start to eat. This is what you will get from that "good fellow" behind the bar. He will take a seltzer bottle and squirt it in your face and yell:—"Hey, there, you guy, we want drinkers, we don't want eaters. Now you beat it on or I'll give you a bat in the belfry." And that saloon soup is made of noodles, poodles and cayoodles, seasoned with cockroaches, bugs and flies. If you want a taste of this good fellowship drop in any saloon and tackle the lunch, without buying.

Other defenders of a saloon say:—"The great majority of those who patronize the saloon are not attracted thither by its liquors, but by its recreative features." Yes, that's true. If you walk into a saloon, grab a hunk of free lunch and

How can whiskey drown trouble when it will not drown a snake?

don't buy, you will have more recreation than Jess Willard. The bartender or bouncer will have you by the back of the neck and seat of the trousers and if you don't go through a plate glass door, it's because the door is open. Oh, yes! you are welcome in a saloon, if you are broke, just as welcome as a barrel house bum in the White House.

The most abominable and manhood destroying pests in the country to my mind are the saloons and bars tucked away in "respectable" office buildings known as "snake holes!"

A so-called respectable, moderate drinking citizen can sneak in one of these buildings, ostensibly on business. He is not seen entering a saloon by his associates. In high class office buildings in all leading American cities these "snake holes" are starting thousands of men, young and old, on the road to the barrel house, slums and destruction. I will say, however, that all office buildings do not contain these "snake

An overdrawn nature account and bank account spell failure.

holes," as I could name fifty in Chicago, New York, Boston, Philadelphia, and other cities that will not lease space for a "snake hole!" Possibly those who read this can locate office buildings in their respective localities that permit the existence of these vile holes. Many who patronize these places are considered model men in their home community, often being closely allied with churches, civic bodies, and charitable societies, for uplifting and supporting those who are cursed by the burden of drink; reformers and philanthropists in the eyes of the world, but hypocrites and sneaks and cowards in the eyes of their Master. These "snake holes" are the fountain head of drunkenness.

I have met hundreds of saloon keepers who were mean and grasping, absolutely devoid of all love of humanity, men who care nothing for their fellow being so long as they get the "coin." The "death bell" on the cash register is music in their ears.

Every "day of grace" for the saloon is a disgrace.
Take a pony of brandy and ride to destruction

MY LAST DRINK

I know thousands of men engaged in the saloon and whiskey business, having spent a fortune in making their acquaintance. The most of them are prosperous, have comfortable and beautiful homes, live easily, have all the good things of this life, and seem happy. They live in luxury because of the weakness of the poor man who cannot resist the temptation to use their goods. They are living on the blood money wrung from the hearts of wives and children. Does the saloon keeper have any pangs of remorse as he rides through the streets in a richly equipped auto, with his diamond bedecked wife and well dressed and nourished children, and sees some of his bedraggled and besotted victims hobbling along the street? He lives a life of luxury from the destruction of these very people.

Saloon keepers know the goods they sell will produce these results. They are case hardened. They reason it is a legitimate business or the municipality would not legalize it.

A boozer is the one-legged man in the race of life.
Whiskey and war are twins.

MY LAST DRINK

When a saloon keeper orders a few barrels of booze from the distiller, does he stop to think of how much misery he is adding to the community? How many curses he is heaping upon himself; of how many heartaches and tears he is causing; of how many men and families each barrel will ruin? Then let Mr. Saloon Keeper think of his wife and little ones who are made comfortable through the distress of his neighbors and the heart blood of human beings.

The many elements of evil fascination that are about a saloon hold many men and youths in a vise-like grip.

Saloons must have fresh drinking boys every day, or they must go out of business for lack of patronage. The saloon keeper cares nothing for the ultimate effect of drink on his customers or their children or families. A fresh drinking boy every day is necessary to make the saloon cash register ring musically in the saloon proprietor's ears. Wretched men and saddened women and

A saloon keeper's friendship is like the tide; when you are all in, he's out.

orphaned children are living testimonials of the devastating work of saloons. For the groans and heartaches of wives he cares nothing. Fill up the ranks with fresh drinkers and let the old paralyzed and emaciated soaks fill the hospitals, graves, jails, asylums and poor houses. The perpetuation of the saloon business is based on minors forming the habit of liquor drinking at the earliest possible age.

It is not right for any man to derive a living from that which is debasing the minds and ruining the souls of men. No man has a moral or should be given a legal right to sell a poison which produces misery and madness; which is destroying the happiness of the domestic circle, ruining homes and families and filling the land with women and children in a far more deplorable condition than that of widows and orphans; which causes nearly all the crime and pauperism that exists and which the law abiding and sober citizenshp must pay for.

The best way to conquer whiskey is to shun it.
Safety first is sobriety first.

MY LAST DRINK

The liquor traffic is the same unrighteous trade everywhere. It multiplies want, aggravates misery, and stimulates every evil passion into crime. The sufferings of its victims, the poverty, hunger, nakedness, and cold of families, and the battered body—with mind beclouded and conscience destroyed—of the victim, makes a horrible picture.

It is impossible to exaggerate, impossible truthfully to paint the effects of this evil, either on those who are addicted to it, or those who indirectly suffer from it.

Incredible as it may seem to the decent citizen who is not informed in the matter, the tough saloons, barrel houses, pool rooms, and cheap cabarets have formed a working organization and are enabled to exert considerable influence in local politics through swinging the bums and lodging house vote to "favorite sons." If the saloon keeper gets in trouble he appeals to the organization, and they in turn go to the law-

Whiskey causes your old friends to rush by you like a pay car passing a tramp.

yer and politician who are there to protect them in any villainy they may be charged with. A saloon keeper always appeals to his brewer for protection whenever in trouble, and the more of that particular brewery "slop" he sells the more protection and influence he is able to exact from that source.

You can readily see that the saloon and the use of intoxicating drinks is a greater destroying force to life and health and virtue than all other physical evils combined, and all attempts to regulate it will not only prove abortive but will aggravate the evil. Saloons do not need regulation, they need strangulation. They must be eradicated, not a root or germ must be left behind, for until this is done the door of temptation and destruction is wide open to the youth and manhood of the country.

The way of the transgressor is hard, but the path of the saloon keeper is going to be harder.

If it were possible in every instance to determine with precision the responsible causes for all the crimes committed and all the misery suffered by unfortunate men and women it would be found that in an overwhelming majority of cases the saloons and their output would be at fault. It is inconceivable that society should much longer tolerate the existence of an institution that is a social crime. Viewed from the standpoint of economics the saloon is a parasite. It absorbs much and yields nothing. No person is benefited by its existence. The so-called license or revenue it pays is negligible in comparison with the cost it exacts. It is the most destructive agency of which man has knowledge. Even war is not to be compared with it in the ruin it inflicts, for huge as is the waste of war and frightful as is the suffering it occasions, war is periodical, whereas the liquor traffic of the country is continuous in its devastation.

The license system of raising money does not put the burden on the saloon keeper, but places

Sobriety stands for law, order, peace, health and happiness.

the load on the poor and unfortunate booze
fighter. The saloon keeper has no money; if you
don't feed him jitneys and dimes he quits business. He is simply a distress collector for the
municipality in which he conducts his business.
Some people don't seem to care how much crime
and misery and suffering you cause, Mr. Saloon
Keeper. Get all you can, in any way you can,
put up screens so people in the street cannot see
what you do, sell beer in cans and in buckets to
children, short change your customers, don't turn
down a patron because he is ragged and filthy and
you know his family is starving—get the coin.

The liquor traffic stands alone and has no
right to rank with the ordinary avocations of
men. There is no trade so damaging to the people and so hardening to the man engaged in it as
the saloon business. Men naturally kind hearted,
who would help a fellow being in distress, seem
in this trade to lose all humanity and sympathy
in the race for a nickel, even though it is wrung

Whiskey stands for drunkenness, poverty, crime, vice and
scores of attendant evils.

from the lifeblood of a brother and at the expense of starving children and heartbroken wives.

The liquor, brewery, and saloon interests of the United States are always active. They seek to control national and local legislation, the press and any agency that can benefit and perpetuate their trade. This combination is as cunning as a fox, wise as a serpent, strong as an ox, bold as a lion, merciless as a tiger, remorseless as a hyena, fierce as a pestilence, deadly as a plague. To condemn and correct such a group is not the pastime of an hour, but the manly, hero-born martyrdom and continuous work of the law abiding and decent citizenship of the country.

CHAPTER SIX

Living With the Underworld

I SPENT months with the real underworld, not only in Chicago, but in cities throughout the country. It is a fact that a whiskey-driven wretch slinks more and more into the lowest haunts and fainter and fainter becomes his vision of decency in attempting to appease his appetite for drink.

Down among the sodden masses of drink bound men I learned for myself, being one of the unfortunate, the awful malignity and curse of whiskey. In a west side saloon one morning I found myself helplessly drunk. After sobering

---

The Liberty Bell's cracked and so is Personal Liberty.
A dry Sunday makes a sober Monday.

---

up a trifle I looked around. Surrounding me was an army of men, babbling and gesticulating. Such a medley of human wreckage stood about me, brought together through drink. I know such a pitiful herd of unfortunates could not be duplicated in any other place in the world but a groggery—the underworld in action.

Here I was at last, drunk, homeless, helpless, one of and among the human machines that put themselves out of order with whiskey. I noted their bloated faces and half nourished bodies, bleared eyes, and vicious countenances, unwashed, ragged, and all clamoring for drink, but in my drunken condition I did not fully realize the depths to which I had reached.

Here in this vermin infected district I practically lived for months. I was as familiar as though born and bred in the place. Every thief, bum, hobo, drunkard, and dope fiend seemed to be a friend, and in my crazed and drunken condition I entered body and soul into their lives. Where

You can't raise American Beauty roses in a beer garden.
A bartender is the advance agent of the devil.

the liquor came from I do not remember, but it was the rankest and vilest stuff that ever passed a man's lips. I was morally dead—from booze. I was going through an awful experience.

The degrading associates, the immoral atmosphere, the sad sights I witnessed, made up a composite picture of sadness and despair that will never be forgotten.

Here were seen all the bitter suffering and utter despair of the men who had played the wrong side of life and were paying the penalty, the finished product of the vile saloon.

Here I met and consorted with many sorts of criminals. My life among them, questioning them, hearing them plan with their confederates for a robbery as carefully as a board of bank directors would consider an application for a loan, I came to understand thoroughly the motives and methods of that criminal portion of the community put down as the underworld. The great mass of people know nothing about this class

Some men boast of being well preserved after a drinking life. They ought to be—they are well pickled.

except that they are law breakers. Nearly every one I met drank whiskey or were dope fiends. Their meetings and conferences and planning were always in a saloon.

With all the desolation and woe about me, I was powerless to break away. I found life with the underworld a cruel and remorseless one. For weeks not a meal passed my lips, nothing but cheap and half cooked food, put out as free lunch in foul and insanitary saloons. I slept in chairs and on benches in saloons a few hours during the day, and if I managed to get a few nickels would get a ten cent bed in a cheap lodging house; failing in this I would walk the streets until the saloons opened at 5 A. M. The only time I was sure of being in out of the cold for a night would be when arrested for some offense and thrown in a police station or the county jail, which occurred many times.

I was not long in learning that all barrel houses and most of the saloons give their un-

A rubber back and a weak mind is the devil's model of a perfect man.

derworld patrons every morning what is known as an "eye opener" or a "brain duster," or "shot of dynamite."

This starts you in for the day. Every bum and whiskey drinker must have a drink in the morning. I would start in South State Street and wind up in Madison Street or Halsted Street, getting a "lifesaver" of poison in nearly every dump. By the time one had worked the system he would be reasonably drunk and ready to commit any deed the mind presented. Thousands are going over the same route in Chicago today, and in other cities throughout the United States, as all groggeries have a similar scheme. These saloon keepers figure that a few drinks will give a bum nerve and he will start out to beg, borrow or steal, and the proceeds will come to his joint.

I was aware in my half sane moments that there was only one end to this life I was living. I would try to restrain myself. A drunkard lives in continual fear of delirium tremens. He

It is about as easy to separate the light and heat of the sun as it is to separate drink and poverty.

cares nothing for death.   I was gradually going down the scale.

I was living in a world which knew nothing of decency, sobriety, honor, or self-respect. Such things as the thought of a former beautiful home a few blocks from this cesspool of degradation was a vague and unregarded recollection. I wanted drink—and more drink.   Can you conceive of such a world on West Madison Street, within a stone's throw of the beautiful Northwestern Railway Station?   Of course not!   There it was, and there it is today.   Yet I lived there and associated with thousands of poor wretches, many of whom, like myself had seen better days, but the everlasting crave for drink had pinioned them to destruction.   I drank with these men, begged with them, slept with them, in cheap lodging houses, trucks and cellarways.   Sober enough to read sometimes, I would muddle over a newspaper.   Wars, great political changes, deaths, catastrophes, these events were utterly dull and

A boozer's life is like a checker board with old John Barleycorn always in the King Row.

insignificant to me.   I was always wondering where I could get another drink.   Everything was gone; I was about ready to strike bottom.

Among the men I met in those hideous holes were many who had been prominent and prosperous in the business and professional life of Chicago—now awful wrecks. Booze was their master.

There was apparently nothing left for me but to push myself hurriedly to a drunkard's grave. Daily some of my new found cronies were being lugged to the morgue, hospital or jail. These things did not feaze me.   I had already been everywhere, but the morgue.   There was no substance, spirit, brain or will power left.   I was a nervous, drunken, alcoholic wreck. Hope, courage, loyalty, truth, I had parted with completely. Everything was blank, it seemed.   I had no ties, I had no friends, I had no home whatsoever, all brought about by myself.   I was aware that whiskey is a mind destroying, body sapping, reputation corroding beverage, but I was powerless to face the other way.

One night I stood on the sawdust floor of a barrel house, drunk, sick, nervous, a motionless wreck, when I was seized with a whiskey fit, and although it was a bitter winter's night, the boss of the joint had me carried out in the alley—little caring whether I froze to death or not. A friendly hobo put me in a lodging house, which undoubtedly saved my life.

I was firmly intrenched in the haven of the underworld, in the Desplaines Police District of Chicago. Here were assembled thousands of shells of men in the saloons, liquor stores and barrel houses. Wickedness and drunkenness were dealt out without stint in this district and with these men there remained only a charred, stupid, indecent thirst for liquor. Here they all congregate—the alcoholic wrecks of the city. Dimly lit, stifling lodging houses, with a "good" bed for ten cents, foul cellar drinking places, thieves' resorts, second-hand dealers and groggeries and barrel houses, were alive with an army of wicked men and boys, and dirt, rags, vermin, blasphemy, booze and darkness reigned without hindrance; a fantastic and ghostly confusion of human derelicts. The condition was not unusual to the police. They would saunter jauntily through this round of drunks, bums, hobos and thieves, and stop at a bright light occasionally, put a "few under their belt" and move along. The conditions on the street and in the saloons were of no moment to them. Thousands of people passing on the street and in street cars and automobiles; streets crowded, and in fact a horrible sight for women, girls and young men to see, the very lowest of saloons and barrel houses soliciting trade, with their front doors wide open.

Nobody seemed to care. It seemed to be taken as an accepted fact that this condition had always existed in the neighborhood and always would. Here I was in the melting pot of this

A snake with every drink is the prize all boozers draw.
A red nose is not caused by eating red apples.

dissipating and disappearing humanity. Ragged and shriveled human forms would shuffle out of sight daily; faces would vanish for the last time and police patrols and ambulances were busy making hurried trips to jails, morgues and hospitals. Nobody cared, nobody remembered any unfortunate companion after the day was over, and I was cognizant of all this hideousness and misery and distress and death and still I was alcoholically welded to these ratholes. But the precision of familiarity made me acquainted with the devious and devilish ways the business of the district was managed, and I often saw a stranger who had been lured to the neighborhood, with money on his person, pushed into a saloon, given a few "knockout" drops in his whiskey become turned around and mystified and stupefied from drink, and then gently "rolled" or robbed and pushed into the alley and picked up by a policeman and "thrown in" for being drunk and asleep in a public place. Nobody cares!

The saloon bar brings many a good man to the bar of justice

MY LAST DRINK

The wonder to the uninitiated is how the great army of loafers and drunks manage to eat, drink, have a place to sleep and garments to clothe themselves in. Each bum has a system he has marked out that gives him an existence. Hundreds of the men who are still fairly normal, whose earlier lives led them in legitimate business channels, are employed during the day addressing envelopes in letter shops, addressing firms, large printing offices, and others who send out printed matter and circulars for local business firms. These are known as "pen dumps." The daily average pay is about seventy-five cents. Coffee and rolls in the morning five cents; two "tubs of suds" and free lunch at noon, ten cents; fifteen cents for a bed, and the balance for supper and booze. The booze is five cents a drink and is known as "five-year-olds," "Kys," or "Ponies." A rotten, doctored, diluted, poisoned decoction that makes a man stupid, crazy and delirious.

This mode of living is closely followed by all

Drink keeps a man right between the hammer and anvil all his life—the saloon keeper is the blacksmith.

the "gin-heads" in the underworld population. "Out on the stem" and "mooching," is the easiest graft a bum can work. In the "one legged saloon" on Halsted Street, about forty cripples made their headquarters. The saloon keeper gave each of them car fare, and about two o'clock every afternoon they would ride out to a residence neighborhood, panhandle from door to door, "stemming" or "mooching" and often they came back with as high as ten dollars in small coin, not one ever returning empty handed. If a stew gets drunk and breaks or loses his crutch this saloon has a supply on hand. They will tie your arm up in bandages to give the appearance of a fracture, furnish you with green or smoked goggles and a cane to feel along with. In fact make you a first-class blind beggar in five minutes.

Others peddle collar buttons, shoe strings, combs, and although they sell an occasional article the goods are carried for a blind. If the house-

A man who follows the bright lights is always in the dark.
Personal Liberty is organized hypocrisy.

MY LAST DRINK

wife is not on guard and the front door unlocked, Mr. Peddler will pick up a clock, vase, piece of statuary, rug or anything that can be sold. Old bums and drunks are continually begging clothes. If they can't use them, to the secand-hand store they go, or to some ragged pal.

I tried to quit drinking, but only for a day. But I was helpless and hopeless, and finally I found my way back to the barrel house district where many a poor drunken wretch, with a broken heart from repeated failures, had gone before me, and for months I lived there a homeless drunken vagabond, eking out a living by begging, borrowing, and passing worthless checks. There are hundreds of saloons in Chicago with a flaming sign over the door, "Workingmen's Exchange." Yes, it is an exchange, where a poor devil exchanges his brains and money for booze and misery.

Just for drink! I didn't want food. What does a drunken bum want with food? A crumb

The man in the moon would not be a very profitable saloon customer. He gets full only once a month.

82

or two of free lunch; it's as much as a man's stomach will hold—what I wanted was another drink, a little more alcohol on the fire. Then the next drink. I pursued it for years—growing weaker mentally, physically, always hoping for a mirage of soul's care. It is labor to pursue the next drink forever. But exhaustion is stupid and numb. I slept or rested but little—snatches here or there in a barrel house, or cheap saloons or cheap lodging houses until thrown out; nobody wanted a drunk around; even the villainous saloon keeper who fills you with poison will throw you out if you are too noisy or broke.

I was successful at drinking, successful enough to have the delirium tremens twice.

I was systematic in my hunt for drink. I could not and would not work. I was too sick, nervous and physically worthless. I carried a little memorandum in my pocket and I would map out my itinerary from day to day, beginning at State and Randolph in the morning and winding

MY LAST DRINK

up at Thirty-first and State about midnight, good and drunk. Different streets on different days was my program. I must not panhandle the same saloon twice the same week or there would be trouble; they might kick me out. I would go to bed full and get up in the morning with only a general idea of where I had ended my previous day's work, and if I called on the same saloon, trouble would ensue and out I would go, very kindly assisted by the bartender, who did not request me to call again.

Hundreds of my companions were sent to the Bridewell. Out for a while and in again. The short confinement did no good. Society should change its attitude toward those sentenced for acts committed while under the influence of alcohol. If we simply shut up drunkards, and only remove the alcohol for the time being, you do not obtain an essential improvement of their nature. The prison penalty should be supplanted by a thorough and serious education on the evils of

A home is a vested right; a saloon a vested wrong.
Whiskey is the devil in liquid form.

drink.   Men must be taught that alcohol is their destroyer, but no penal or moralizing teaching is going to reform any one.   Instead, they must, according to capacity, be given a thorough knowledge of the effects of alcohol upon the mind and body.

CHAPTER SEVEN

Suffering From Delirium Tremens

THE awful penalty of excessive drinking was my lot at last. I was picked up in the street and rushed to a hospital, with that terrible scourge, delirium tremens, gripping my whole system in a vise of writhing agony. It was of my own making. I knew it was coming, but I was weak, had an uncontrollable appetite for whiskey and deliberately plunged myself into this awful condition.

I am making my own terrible experiences and sufferings public as an object lesson to drinkers who are slowly reaching this sure toboggan of

---

If you make a business of drinking booze, booze will get your business.

---

misery.   Let it be known to all that the whole story and history of alcohol is a tragedy.   My experience and observations are given as a beacon light to those who are embarking upon this slippery road.

In the slimy trail of the alcoholic serpent you will find everything that is dark and dreadful.   I found it.

The sight of a man undergoing the terrible tortures of delirium tremens is one I trust no reader of these lines will ever witness.   It would live with you to the day of your death.   God grant that horrible sight may forever be spared you.

What is there in whiskey that enters a man's soul and very life and drags him down to the level of a beast?

I give but a mere outline of the picture of this terrible scourge, which condition, in the fulness of awful detail, God only knows.

I was placed on a cot, stripped and manacled and placed in a straitjacket.   My body writhed

The nation is founded on manhood and womanhood; the saloon is founded and thrives on the wrecks of both.

and trembled and my parched lips had their skin torn as I tried to utter words of condemnation to my attendants who were restraining me. I could plainly see toads squatting in the corners and serpents were coiled about the bed posts, and hissing in my ears, while all manner of imps were dancing about in the air, spouting a blue flame in my face. Such a horrible, torturing condition no man can truly portray or describe. It was as though all the demons of hell had combined to harass and torment me.

In my drunken frenzy I shrieked for alcohol —alcohol in any form. There were days of mental restlessness and nights of sleepless torture.

No chamber of horrors ever described could convey an accurate description of the awful, crucial and soul killing writhings that I experienced. Jumping out of the way of pink elephants, feeling carefully on my bed clothing for gila monsters and lizards, moaning, howling and crying for some unseen force to relieve me from my awful

A saloon keeper is usually a diplomat, but his customers are always doormats.

condition, I would finally lapse into a fit. Occasionally a "shot of dope" would be injected to allay my sufferings, but even with that I would continue to writhe, and curse and spit and glare, my eyeballs bloody and protruding and ablaze with fury.

Hideous faces appeared on the walls and on the ceiling and on the floors; foul things crept along my bedclothes and glaring eyes peered into mine. I was at one time surrounded by myriads of monstrous spiders and rats which crawled slowly, slowly, over every limb, while beaded drops of perspiration would start to my brow, and my limbs would shiver until the bed rattled.

Strange colored lights would dance before my eyes, and then suddenly the very blackness of darkness would appall me by its dense gloom. All at once, while gazing at a frightful creation of my distempered mind, I seemed to be struck with a sudden blindness. I knew an electric light was burning in the room, but I could

Split a bottle of champagne with a saloon keeper and he will usually reciprocate by splitting a bottle of beer.

not see it—all was so pitchy dark. Suddenly I saw standing at the foot of my bed a red devil with hands polluted with blood and arms filled with serpents that were crawling and wriggling, and stinging and hissing, for their unpitying and unrelenting master. My very vitals were pierced with agony as the red monster continued to jeer and taunt and pursue his infernal work. Is there no escape from this terrible torture, I moaned. It would seem as though nothing but death could give me relief, and oh! how welcome it would have been.

To somewhat alleviate my pain the attendant released my arms for a few minutes. All at once I lost the sense of feeling. As I tried to grasp my arm in one hand the sense of touch was gone. I put my hand to my side, my head, but felt nothing, and still I knew my limbs, my frame, were there. And then the scene would change. I was falling—falling, swiftly as an arrow—far down into some terrible abyss; and so realistic

A saloon cash register is the devil's chime. Just place a coin in the snake's mouth and hear it ring.

was it, as I fell, I could see the rocky sides of the horrible shaft, where mocking, gibing, fiend-like forms were perched, and I could feel the air rushing past me, making the sweat stream out by the force of the unwholesome blast. Then the paroxysm sometimes ceased for a few moments, and I would sink back on my pallet drenched with perspiration, utterly exhausted, and feeling a dreadful certainty of the renewal of my torments.

There were times when it seemed absolutely impossible to stand the strain for another minute.

At times the torture would return and slimy, gliding, writhing, biting, stinging adders would wind themselves about my body and thrust their forked and poisonous tongues into my sides.

My eyes were bleared and glistening and pain and fright enthralled me, and I prayed and begged and entreated that death might relieve me.

Not one man in one hundred thousand could go through my experience and emerge with life.

A shot of booze has wounded many a man to his death.
All saloon keepers argue that a fly is a pest.

MY LAST DRINK

I was not the only victim in my ward suffering with this awful curse.

I could hear the crackling flames of burning victims and the shrieks of suffering men. Around their dying beds could be seen serpents unfolding coil after coil from out of the darkness, brandishing their forked tongues to sting them and lick their blood as a fierce flame licks up its fuel.

And some in their agony begged to be let plunge into a lake of fire to escape still greater torture; others would stand on their cot shrieking with agony and begging their attendants to plunge them to death to escape further awful tortures. Demoniacal ravings, mutterings and curses made a perfect bedlam of the ward; the whole a human tragedy terrible to witness. Others were moaning and crying, shrieking and cursing and dying, while several were uttering the most heart-piercing and piteous prayers for death to relieve them that ever passed the lips of man.

Don't forget that advertised whiskey without "A headache in it," contains many heartaches.

MY LAST DRINK

Even now these terrible combats come at me like a nightmare and are often re-enacted in ghostly pantomime in my sleep.

One poor victim, formerly a well-known Chicago business man, was on his knees with his hands clasped in prayer, his eyes looking upward, shrieking that death might come at once to relieve him, which it did.

The most impressive and saddest sight of all I witnessed was to see young men scarcely out of their teens, chained to cots and beds, suffering with delirium tremens; some good mother's boy who had been caught and pinioned in the horrible grip of drink.

The deaths from delirium tremens throughout the United States annually is said to be approximately fifty thousand. The total of those who die from acute alcoholism and other forms of alcoholic dissipation, added to the above, would reveal an aggregate that would astound everyone.

All these horrors have sprung from a cause

Mr. Moderate Drinker, John Barleycorn is quietly electrocuting you in the chair of booze.

that is perfectly curable, that is easily remediable and absolutely preventable.

Mr. Whiskey Drinker, just keep up your present batting average of drink and that day is not far distant when you will be a "jim jam" boy, yourself.

The saloon is a malignant, disease-spreading nuisance, causing death, misery and desolation throughout the length and breadth of the country. What do these saloon traffickers care if a few thousand patrons die annually from delirium tremens, alcoholism, and its attendant evils? What do they care if thousands of children are annually thrown on the charity of the public? What do they care for the misery and distress caused by drink?

Look in every direction in the United States. You will see the frightful, intolerable evidences of the devastation of drink.

The drink traffic is the cause of most of the crimes committed; causes an amazing waste of

Whiskey with a sting and a rattlesnake's sting both have the same effect.

national resources, both physical and human. Pauperism is its offspring; it causes the great majority of divorces and other domestic difficulties which fill our police courts; it is the advance agent of the social evil; causes thousands of premature deaths, chokes our prisons, penitentiaries, jails, insane asylums, reformatories, and hospitals; and sentences thousands of miserable men and yet more miserable women and pitiable children to lead most wretched lives.   It blights the body and soul of all who drink it, is the chief bane and ruin of thousands of homes and is today the one black spot and stain on the glory, prosperity and freedom of the greatest republic the world has ever known.

CHAPTER EIGHT

Life in Barrel Houses and Cheap Lodging Houses

A BARREL house and a cheap lodging house are twins. Where one exists the other lives. They are the twin devils of crime and debauchery.

As I dropped lower in the scale of life I naturally gravitated to the barrel house. My physical condition was on a par with my mental calibre. My step was slow and unsteady. My will power was completely gone. You could readily see that I was a bum. It was on a bitter cold day I made my first visit to a barrel house. I had on summer clothes, such as they were, a ragged coat

---

Saloon keepers are in favor of having women at the polls—
at the North and South poles.

---

and pants all frazzled. My nose was the size and color of a big ripe plum, garnished with whiskey blossoms.

And there I stood and such a pitiable object of despair and misery, no artist could depict. I was surrounded by a lifeless, insipid mob of unwashed, hungry and thirsty men. I did not know that such human beings existed—but there they were in a barrel house saloon, right in the heart of Chicago, and this was only one of hundreds of similar rat holes in the city.

Sin, vice, crime, filth, drunkenness, miserable squalor and wretchedness, poverty and disease, degradation, and in fact, every kind of conceivable wickedness met me on every hand.

There is a great cry raised about the barrel house by the so-called better or respectable saloon. There is no difference in any of them. A drunkard does not form the drinking habit in one of these holes. He forms the habit by drinking in a "respectable" saloon, club or hotel

When sowing your wild oats don't mix too much rye with them.

MY LAST DRINK

bar.   A barrel house is the last stop you make
on your way to the grave.   It is the only drink
hole that will tolerate a down and out.   Drunkards are not made in barrel houses—just the
finished product wind up there.

You can get a "tub of suds" and a "plate,"
a bit of lunch, for a nickel.   Whiskey is five
cents a drink.   They are known as "Ky's,"
"Ponies" and "Five-Year-Olds."   The beer is
the cheapest slop made, and how and from what
the booze is made, no one knows—that is, those
who drink it.   This barrel house booze is stupe-
fying and will make a normal man crazy.   As long
as you have a "jitney" you are not refused a drink.
If you get too drunk and are boisterous or ugly,
out you go, head first.   Chairs are arranged
along the wall for guests and if a "live one"
drops in he is pounced upon to "buy."   The
proprietor encourages this procedure, as he figures every nickel helps him.   The average barrel
house free lunch is made up of an undesirable

A distiller has for a trademark a bee hive.   That means
his product stings his customers.

98

mixture of scraps and junk, highly seasoned and "embalmed" meats and fish and alfalfa soup, that a starving dog would turn his back on. But a drunken man will grab it with the same enjoyment a sober man would eat turkey at a wedding feast.

When a man begins to treat his organs as though they were the works of a dollar watch evil is bound to result.

Drink led me to these low and filthy haunts, the vilest quarters in the world, where mendicancy and drunkenness and vice are entwined together; where the most depraved and brutish of men mete out the destructive drug to haggard want and tattered wickedness for the poor price of a nickel, which often has been snatched by theft or begged on the street.

For a scene of horrid vice and filth and distress and fury and faces of debauched and wicked men, all drawn into the horrible vortex and there fermenting and seething in misery

The booze route is a short and crooked one and the bell rings every time you start.

and disease, a man might search the world all over and not find a rival to the cheap saloons and barrel houses on West Madison and North and South State and Clark Street and the neighboring streets. Why the police and health department allow them to exist no one knows. Maybe the brewers and distillers who always manage to get a strangle hold on the business could answer the question. I found the same conditions existing in all large American cities.

I lived among these conditions for a long time. I drank the whiskey, partoook of the lunch, and slept on a chair when permitted. I would go out on the street occasionally, beg a few nickels from old friends, then shuffle back to some low groggery, beg or buy a drink, or run into a live one (a bum who had a little change). I would hang around a saloon until closing time, one o'clock, and then be thrown out in the street; nowhere to go, no home, no bed, nothing; walk the streets until 5 o'clock in the morning. Then

As a saloon keeper rises in power and splendor his patrons sink in squalor and want.

the saloons open again. All first comers are given the regular "Eye Opener" or "Brain Duster," and a bowl of soup. I would then grab a chair and go to sleep. In a couple of hours along would come the bouncer, and, welting me across the back with a rubber hose, order me out for a new bunch of down and outs who wanted to sleep; two hours for them and out they go; and this goes on all day. This was my life day after day, week after week. A great army of men are going through the same routine in all of the large cities of the United States today, and particularly in Chicago they run way up in the thousands.

The great majority of people know nothing about how this army of floaters exists, and under what conditions they flourish. A tramp, hobo, bum and beggar are all alike. The only difference is the smell. The general public pictures this class as nothing more than drunken, shiftless, ragged fugitives trying to dodge work, content

A saloon keeper who wears a diamond is not a gem.
The best way to conquer booze is to shun it.

to tramp aimlessly from town to town and subsist upon cold victuals begged from door to door. But as a fact the strongest instinct in a hobo's life, as seen in Chicago, New York, and large centers of population, is to eke out a living without rendering compensation in labor. From first to last the hobo is voluntarily and premeditatedly a parasite, a sponging vagrant, the man of all men who never works, and never will. Once he goes to work he ceases to be a hobo.

In the saloons, barrel houses, and lodging houses throughout the city I found a cosmic population representing nearly every country in the world. The most were unskilled in a trade, or illiterate, or both. They all drank whiskey. If they had any education at all it was only in the most rudimentary sense. When it was whispered about that I was a former Alderman I was looked upon as a man of influence and when in trouble they would appeal to me for advice, and my advice would be along the lines that would net me

Many tombstones in cemeteries are monuments to the saloon traffic.

a drink the quickest. These vagabonds all lived a life of chance, the same as I did, and had no occupation. I soon learned that all chronic hangers-on in pool rooms, saloons, barrel houses and cheap "flops" are an improvident, debauched, whiskey soaked, meandering band of worse than helpless men. They hang out in those vile saloons called "Workingmen's Home" which in reality is a "Workingmen's Morgue."

A saddening sight was to gaze upon the hundreds of gloomy men in the evening of old age, starving, storming and begging for whiskey in saloons, and food at missions and in bread lines; with mind and memory dead, physically broken down and crippled, waiting for the wagon or ambulance to back up and close their book of life.

I wish every man and woman could see these things as I have seen them, and as they exist to-day. Then it would not take long to sweep from the country the primary cause—whiskey.

The raw material used to perpetuate the whiskey business is young men and boys.

MY LAST DRINK

There is a natural bond of sympathy that draws all these tramps, bums, hobos, thieves and ex-convicts together, a bond that is hard for the rest of the world to understand or appreciate. The underworld is loyal to its own.

Did you ever sleep in a cheap Chicago lodging house? No! Well, you are lucky. There is a lodging house capacity in Chicago for 100,000 men, and these "Palaces" are mainly patronized by the intemperate, criminal and shiftless class, presenting in many ways the worst elements of our population.

The cell type of room is used in most places and the price of a bed is from 10 to 25 cents. A cell room is about 6x10. The floor is cement. The side walls are about 7 feet in height, are usually corrugated iron, in some instances being wood. The bed is an iron frame affair, a thin mattress and something they call a sheet, pillow and blanket is there, if you wish to use them. These rooms are arranged in long rows from

When the liquor interests thrive, the people suffer.
All are equal before the awful scourge.

the front of the building to the rear, the only ventilation coming from the top of the cell, which is covered with a strong wire netting.

When one retires he places the bed against the door for safety. It is good policy to hide your clothes under your mattress so that some "guest" will not raise the roof of wire netting and fish up your wardrobe, which is easily accomplished by placing a nail in a broom. Robberies are frequent, but a wise man sleeps with his clothes on. These rooms are usually dark, damp, ill-ventilated and vermin infected. One night a man infected with small pox or tuberculosis may occupy a room and next night a young man from the country is given the same bed. The "linen" in a first-class lodging house is changed whenever the bedmaker, usually some drunken bum, thinks it advisable. On each floor are toilet and washing facilities that in most cases even a tramp will not use. I will not attempt to describe the bath tub.

The history of alcoholism is tragedy, murder, starvation and death.

MY LAST DRINK

Every lodging house in Chicago gets filled with vermin and dirt, and twice a year every guest is routed out and the places fumigated and all crawling guests "smoked out."

There is a police, fire, and sanitary regulation of lodging houses, and in the months I was a guest at nearly every one in the city, I never saw or heard of an inspector in any one of them.

I was once pushed out of a West Side barrel house, which was an all night haunt for drunkards, and went to "Hogan's Flop," which is close to the Desplaines Street Police Station, where one may sleep for five cents. There every night are herded hundreds of men, packed in a large barn-like room on the bare floor, with a newspaper for a blanket, like pigs in a stock train. I spent a few nights in "Hogan's" and such a motley mass of humanity was never marshalled before. Singing, shouting, snoring, and blasphemy was the regular program. No man dare take off his clothes or shoes, for if you slept too soundly one of the guests would appropriate your wardrobe and walk off.

It is conditions such as I have enumerated that are giving the saloons a black eye. Thousands of drinking men are growing to hate the whole business, and the way it is conducted, and despairing of ever seeing a better condition of regulation have concluded that the only way to get back at it is to put it entirely out of existence. Another thing influencing such men is the awful nature of the beer and whiskey sold over the bar. It has changed for the worse in the last few years. A New York bartender who has grown grey and crippled in the business informed me that beer would not keep through the day in a barrel; that they had to be extremely careful to order only the exact amount necessary for if they had only one keg too much it would spoil. Another said to me, "I sell beer all day, but I never drink a glass of it. It isn't fit for a white man to drink." This man was not in a barrel

The moderate drinker is the great stumbling block in the path of prohibition.

107

house or slum dive, but in one of the best saloons in the heart of Boston.

The barrel house and low saloon dive is the spot that all men drop to and seek when in the final beggary of hopeless drunkenness. They are cast out from men, loathsome, despised and perishing. It is a shocking, awful sight to see those poor, unfortunate human beings, on the last lap of their existence. I have seen scores of men drop dead in different barrel houses and saloons and hustled to the morgue in a most mechanical manner. Nobody cared. They were used to such scenes. It might be them next. They didn't care. All rushed to a drunkard's grave, without a prayer, uncoffined, unwept and unknown. The same conditions exist today. Nobody cares.

CHAPTER NINE

Police, Police Courts, Police Stations and Jails

THE happiest, proudest, grandest moment in a policeman's life is when he can "pinch" a fellow man, walk up to the patrol box, call up the station and say: "This is McCasey. Send the wagon to Harrison and State street at once. Have a desperate divil in tow."

McCasey has a poor, drunken bum by the collar. The crowd grows. McCasey yells, "G'wan, move 'long, there," swinging his club threateningly at the mob. The wagon arrives. In goes the drunk. McCasey yells, "Book this man for disorderly conduct." Up the street he

Sunday closing is an "eye opener" for the saloon keepers. A seasoned drinker makes poor business timber.

struts.   At ten next morning the clerk of the police court yells, "John Jones and Officer Mc-Casey."

The Judge—"What's this man charged with?"

The Clerk—"Disorderly conduct."

Officer McCasey—"Sign a waiver."

This waiver means you will be tried at once by the presiding judge and you waive your rights to a jury trial.

The Clerk—"Be sworn."   Jones and officer are sworn.

Officer McCasey—"I found this man yelling in front of a saloon at Harrison and State Streets and he was arguing with a dago about the price of bananas, creating a great disturbance, and attracting a crowd. I told him to move along. He said he was an American citizen and called me a furriner and stiff."

The Judge—"Had you been drinking, Jones?"

Everyone plugs a rat role. Why not a drink hole?
Drink lashes a man to the mast of destruction.

MY LAST DRINK

John Jones—"Yes, sir; I had been in 'Hinky Dink's' joint and had two 'tubs of suds,' but I wasn't drunk, your honor."

Officer McCasey—"Your honor, he was drunk, sor, and when I told him to move, he resisted me."

The Judge—"In what way did he resist you?"

Officer McCasey—"He said he would not allow any 'bull neck' to order him around when he was minding his own business."

John Jones—"I have worked steadily for two years as a laborer for the Crane Company; was never arrested in my life, and the officer clubbed and struck me, and I have laid in this rotten, louse-bound Clark Street Police station since yesterday noon, a dry crust of bread to eat, with muddy water they called coffee, to drink, and the lockup keeper would not notify my family or friends. Your honor, the officer was half-stewed himself."

Big Business is using a big club and is effectually batting booze.

MY LAST DRINK

Officer McCasey—"I have seen this man in State Street before, and always drunk."

John Jones—"I was never drunk in my—"

The Judge—"That'll do, Jones, you are a dangerous man, a menace to society, and the sooner men like you are put away the better for the community.   I think about six months in the Bridewell will make a good citizen of you."

The Clerk—"Horace Johnson and Officer Robinson."   And this is the way it goes from day to day in all the police courts of Chicago.   No friends, no pull, with the police knocking and pounding, on you go.   A policeman's reputation for efficiency is based on the number of arrests he makes, and if he is lucky enough to convict some one he will get special commendation from his superior officers.   The Cossacks of Russia have nothing on many men on the police force of Chicago.   The club and the concealed, but too readily handy gun, are still the signs by which a policeman conquers.

"Will you have a drink?" is not asked by employers today, but, "Do you drink?"

MY LAST DRINK

A plain clothes man can stop any citizen on the street, night or day, ask an array of insulting questions, "frisk you," (search your pockets), give you a kick or a push and tell you to beat it. A man thus accosted is naturally incensed, makes some pretty sharp replies and says, "Who are you?" Then the plain clothes man will throw open his coat, exhibit his star, and say:

"I'm an officer. Don't give me any of your lip or I'll run you in. Good notion to do it anyway. Where do you live? What's your name? What are you doing in this neighborhood?"

The citizen is angry, confused and scared, and if he is imprudent enough to ask the officer his number or name he is liable to get a slam in the mouth. Thousands of respectable Chicago citizens have had this experience and are still having it, every day in the year.

There ought to be some law or measure to correct the present evils of the police force. A

Drink and graft are the twin evils of the century.
A boozer never fools anyone but himself.

policeman does not regard his position as a post of responsibility, but as a piece of property. No matter how inefficient, undisciplined, barbarous or corrupt he may be he feels he is under the protecting wing of the civil service, usually has some unseen political pull, and always manages to keep his grip on his position unless he is convicted before a court of law.

The police should be like an army, the responsive instrument of a leader, then if there were corruption the people would know whom to blame; if efficiency results the people would know whom to trust and commend.

If we could by some means constitute all the members of the police force agents for the social betterment of the city, what an influence for good they might exert—and this without any diminution of their authority as officers of the law. They are today, almost without exception, men of medium calibre, each man using his own judgment, club or gun at any time or place he sees fit. He

The man behind the gun in war is not more deadly than the man behind the bar in peace.

figures that he is clothed with power—why not use it?

A policeman is the same whether in Chicago, or New York, Kankakee, or Podunk.   A star, a gun, a club, has the same effect on the human mind made up of police material the world over. Of 130,000 arrests made in Chicago during twelve months, one-half were discharged, which shows how much common sense is used in "running in" citizens. If it were not for the good judgment of the Municipal Court Judges the police would have one-half of the population of Chicago continually in jail.

I will say, however, that I was courteously treated by all policemen and police officials. But what I saw and learned of police system and authority was a revelation.

The most pernicious parody on humanitarianism ever evolved by the mind of man are the barbarous, foul-smelling, vermin-infected, ill-ventilated garbage boxes, called cells, in the

MY LAST DRINK

Chicago police stations, and they are to be avoided like poison. Positive neglect and insult is the order in all of them and it is not hearsay with me, as I was a "guest" in most of them. I was locked up at the Central Station, in La Salle Street near Randolph. I was put in a cell at three o'clock, P. M., having been arrested for passing a worthless check, to procure money for whiskey. I was put in a cell about 8 by 10, with a plank bed on either side, no bedding of any kind, no water, and disgraceful toilet facilities. A cup of cold water was shoved in about eight o'clock, nothing to eat, but fortunately I had a little change. I gave an attendant fifty cents to purchase me a sandwich. He returned in about five minutes with an egg sandwich that he must have had in stock. The bread was like rubber and the egg was certainly made of asbestos. I asked him for my change, all the money I had in the world. He replied, "I'm no errand boy, and if you wasn't a

---

"Free drinks and free soup" are the mirages of hope for a down and out.

116

piker you wouldn't ask for change." If you ever think you are going to be locked up have your change in nickels and pennies and carry them in your shoes.

At five o'clock a ragged, dirty, vermin-infected old man was placed in the cell with me; then two young boys about 15 and 17 came in for "sassing" an officer; at nine o'clock in came two more drunks and a holdup man. The adjoining cell was filled with a howling, drunken mob of men. By twelve o'clock eleven men were huddled in my cell. At each new arrival the lockup keeper would rattle his bunch of keys, ram the cell door with a bang; officers, desk sergeants, and hangers on in the office near the cells were talking, whistling, laughing. There was no sleep for anyone. Nobody cared. Nobody tried to maintain order. If you wanted anything to eat, or a friend called on the telephone, you paid for it. You don't get anything for nothing in a police station but an ugly look, and curt reply and a "rap in the jaw"

The sober public has the number of every drinking man.
A tramp is the finished product on parade.

---

if you talk back. The brave policeman has you in his toils and if you are wise you will govern yourself accordingly.

A well-dressed, middle aged man was thrown in about one o'clock, picked up at Madison and Dearborn Streets because he looked "suspicious" to a policeman. After ten minutes residence he yelled: "My God, what a hell hole of a place." He was kept until morning, was never booked, and turned out. This is a favorite pastime of policemen—locking a man up for a few hours and letting him go without booking any charge against him. It seems almost a crime that a policeman is vested with such power, and there ought to be some way to make the municipality responsible for the damage, disgrace and humiliation a citizen is often subjected to.

There are forty-five precinct station jails, the detective bureau jail, the county jail and the Bridewell in the city of Chicago. Of these jails only about a dozen are fit for habitation. Nineteen are underground. Through eleven runs an open sewer. This sewer is a trough flushed by running water. It represents the toilet facilities. When there are more than two persons in a cell they must sleep on the floor beside the open sewer. Frequently eight or ten men are herded together in a cell ten feet square or smaller.

It ought not to require any argument to convince any fair minded man that the municipality has no right to impair or shatter the health of those who are unfortunate enough to be thrown into a police station. The cells should have sunlight and pure, fresh air and prisoners should be protected against disease breeding germs and given modern sanitary conditions. The only humane and sanitary police stations I was locked in were in Pittsburg, Pa., and Los Angeles, Cal. In New York, Philadelphia, Boston, Baltimore and other eastern cities the jail conditions were fair. But who cares? Ninety per cent of all inmates I met were victims directly and indirectly

An intoxicated man is not fit company for man or beast.
Booze and bamboozle are twins of trouble.

of alcohol. Knock strong drink out of any community and note how quickly police stations, jails, prisons, and penitentiaries will show an amazing falling off in population.

A lockup keeper or policeman who has even a drop of human kindness in his system is more than rare. The average policeman thinks everybody except himself is dishonest or a crook, and he deals for so brief a time with individuals, that the formation of the customary links of human kindliness is impossible. The worst characters frequently return, the best stay a short time, are discharged and lost sight of, so a "copper" figures that any act of kindness meets apparently with no reward.

The police, and especially the "dicks," (detectives and plain clothes men), have stool pigeons and squealers in every district in Chicago that they can go to, and unearth nearly any crime they wish. This is evidenced by the fact that when National political conventions are held, or any im-

You will find the "no whiskey" end the better end of life. Walk the straight line and avoid the bread line.

portant personage visits Chicago that means a general outpouring of the people, word goes out to round up all pickpockets, thieves, burglars, confidence men, hotel thieves, etc., for a few days. The police gather them in in short order, know their names, their hangouts and their special line of work.   While known to the police, for the remainder of the year they are allowed to ply their avocations unmolested, unless they get careless or bold and some citizen grabs them.   There is nothing more remarkable in this drama of theft than the perfect understanding which unites the criminal lamb with the wolfish upholder of the law.   The thief looks to his supposed opponent for protection, and looks not in vain as long as he is a fairly good producer and he only gives them up to justice when they fail to yield the coin in abundance.   Nobody cares!

No writer or dramatist that ever lived could depict this situation in its entirety as it exists today and it is a grand tribute to these omnipo-

Only a coward tapers off—a brave man quits abruptly.
A nightcap is a handicap.

tent guardians of law and order and to their human ingenuity, to say that few of them fall below their opportunity, not only in Chicago, but in every city in the United States.

Nature seems to have armed every policeman's hand against his fellows. He seems to be to the manner born and built upon oppression. Policemen are not made, they are born—it's a disease.

What is it in the life and atmosphere of America which encourages and protects crime, or rather elevates crime to a level of excellence unknown elsewhere?

I met a pickpocket in the Warren Avenue police station who had been arrested at Madison and Kedzie avenues. He said a policeman had doubled crossed him and let English Dan, a well-known pickpocket and two confederates have that neighborhood and the Madison and Kedzie cars.

"My," he said to me, "a lot of 'bulls' in this district wouldn't be wearing diamonds if we didn't

John Barleycorn is chasing thousands "Over the Hills to the Poor House."

help pay for them.   They'd sit down in some
saloon and actually cry.   He won't book me. I've
got the goods on him and he knows it."   He wasn't
booked, either.   He was released in a couple of
hours and went with a couple of officers who said
he was wanted in a saloon a few blocks
east of the station.   I met him a few weeks later
and he was "working pockets" on State Street,
and said:

"I'm doing pretty well, thank you."   This
young man considers his business legitimate.   He
intimated that he pays to operate.   The man of
the underworld figures, and not without reason,
that a good many police officers are a far
greater menace to the community than the criminal, and some recent police convictions give
weight to the opinion voiced by crooks.

I spent a few weeks in the Cook county jail
and I found the same criminal atmosphere and
aspect here as in other restraining institutions.
Two and three men were crowded in small, foul

Many men who habitually fool themselves, are a joke to
their acquaintances.

123

smelling cells, the sanitary condition of which ought to receive a little attention from the health department.

Daily from nine-thirty to eleven-thirty, A. M., and from one-thirty to three-thirty P. M., seven or eight hundred inmates are ushered into the Bull Pen for exercise. This is a barn-like room, about 250 feet long and 40 feet wide and here for four hours daily crooks of all kinds meet and talk and plot, without hindrance. There you may meet the murderer, the heat of passion in which he committed his crime forgotten, tranquil, penitent, and self-possessed; the thief, swindler, pickpocket—with all their wits about them—the burglar, holdup man, and forger. All these and hundreds of young men just edging to manhood, locked up upon some petty charge, listening to the wonderful recitals of these hardened and habitual crooks. This Cook county jail bull pen is nothing more or less than a school of instruction for criminals. One young man of twenty-three

Booze has crippled every human being that ever made his acquaintance.

years of age, looking like a boy of seventeen, explained to a group of willing listeners how he worked hotels and robbed guests while they slept; told of how to work transoms without waking any one; told how to get duplicate pass keys from chamber girls in hotels, and how to place your hand under a sleeper's pillow without disturbing him. A pickpocket gave exhibitions of his skill, even picking my pocket while my coat was buttoned tightly. It was so with each adept. Boastful, garrulous, but at the same time imparting a crime knowledge to a class of young men and toughs ready to launch out and give matters a trial. Nobody cares.

It would seem as though all the vice and crime and sin and shame in the community had been jammed into this army of human beings and they were huddled together to instruct each other in their particular line of crime and boast of their awful misdeeds. The enthusiasm some of these men evidenced in giving the details of

A whiskey drinker often wonders why he is at the tail end of the procession. Your friends don't.

their criminal cleverness plainly showed that many possessed ability and talent that would make for success in any legitimate calling.

Society can forgive crime; it will not forgive imprisonment. Whole communities may know that a man is guilty of criminal acts, and he may be punished by heavy fines—yet men and women do not shrink from him—he has been punished, not put in prison. On the other hand the ex-convict is instantly known as such, branded by unmistakable evidences. Sore at society, health shattered, a shifty bearing, a bitter distrust of his fellowmen, no friends or honest acquaintances, and with the police continually picking him up and annoying him, he has no ambition to win back his place in life. He is an outcast. If men learn he has been in prison they refuse to work with him. All mankind instinctively shuns him, not because he has done wrong, but because he has paid the penalty in confinement. When crimes are committed the police sweep through the city and pick

Wake up, Mr. Drinker, and take stock of yourself—a calm, cold, critical inventory—then try to cash it.

up every poor devil that has ever done time, hold him for hours or days as the case may be, without evidence, on the police principle, once a criminal always a criminal. That is not always true, but once a policeman always a policeman is absolutely true.

Many a young man thrown in a pen-like cell in the county jail, owing to inability to secure bail, lays there for months, awaiting indictment and trial. Even if he is released he passes with slow, steady tread out of the jail into freedom feeling that he was wrongfully incarcerated, and across his soul a deep black shadow is photographed against society. He feels that he has been branded a criminal. He goes to the saloon for companionship.

It is only natural, in these circumstances, that he should succumb when a comrade on the street whispers, "You and I are fools to work for a beggarly pittance when we can make a little easy money. Others are doing it everywhere.

Don't gold brick yourself with the delusion that you can quit whenever you want to—you can't do it!

MY LAST DRINK

Look around you, who are the big men in our ward but the saloon keeper and the alderman, and who but them wears diamonds and fancy vests? And how did they make their money? By working hard like you and I? Not in a thousand years!"

Society had imposed on him the conditions that made his fall inevitable. So the problems of crime are world-wide and fundamentally one; and if alcohol and drink is not the father of it all why is it that in communities where drink disappears, crime disappears with it?

CHAPTER TEN

In the Bread Line

WERE you ever in a bread line? No? Well, I was.

At nine-thirty a tramp yelled:—"'The Java Chariot is coming." A ragged, half-drunken, starving, shivering horde of old and young men rushed to the bread line on Jefferson Street as if by magic. The cry of "the Chariot is coming" is relayed to saloons, barrel houses, and lodging houses, throughout the entire Chicago district from Canal and Halsted and Lake Street to Harrison. From dark doorways, alleys, and under-the-sidewalk joints they rush and slink and shuf-

---

Alcohol affects the germ cells and fills the prison cells.
Walk the straight line and avoid the bread line.

fle with all the haste their sodden and stiffened limbs will allow. There I stood in the midst of this motley group of wrecked and drunken humanity, hundreds of whom had seen better days, awaiting my turn to get a cup of coffee and a sandwich. Next in line behind me was a former well-known Chicago merchant, a trembling alcoholic wreck, with scarcely enough vitality to move, and his mind and memory completely shattered from the effects of drink. It was a bitter cold night and before my companion reached the "Chariot" for his hand-out, he fell numb and helpless in the street. A couple of huskies dragged him across the street to the curb and soon the rattle of the "wagon" was heard coming. He was dumped into the patrol wagon as you would throw in a bag of feed, and before the station was reached he was dead. Nobody cared; everybody in the district was daily witnessing similar events.

For nearly two hours several hundred men

In the slimy trail of the alcoholic serpent you will find nothing but worry and misery.

and boys stood in the cold waiting for their "coffee an'," when suddenly the long, slow, shuffling "Bread Line" began to move like a great snake, tattered in garb and spirit. A sight and study is the bread line. Here a young man of twenty, drunk and ragged, there an old man of sixty, pinched and half frozen, stamping with alternate feet upon the sidewalk, others flapping their arms and dancing to keep warm; hundreds of able and brilliant has-beens with bloated faces and bleared eyes, and among them many sober men, honest mechanics, clerks, forced in the line through sickness and industrial conditions, or temporarily embarrassed, and there was also the full quota of out-of-works and never-works from every strata of life.

The Bread Line managers do not preach to the throng, but feed them and wish them good luck and Godspeed.

For an hour the long serpentine line which rolls and unfolds before you grows in length and

When a boozer comes home sober it is a surprise party.
Every day of grace for a saloon is a disgrace.

then you have a clearer impression of the types it contains. It is an amazing aggregation of humanity rather than isolated men. There is the tall man, the short man, and always the old man, the foreigner, professional bum, clerk and boy. The whiskey faces, the unshaven faces, the tightly buttoned coats, the lack of overcoats, the sunken and pale face and slouching knee, with the raven hunger plainly apparent, all these form a composite and pitiful panorama of poverty, with that everlasting stamp of drink, drink, drink, plainly indicated in the features of ninety per cent of them.

I recollect a bitter cold night in the winter of 1914 that again found me in the bread line on Jefferson Street. It was an awful night. There I stood waiting my turn, no overcoat, cracked shoes, with sleet in the air and slush on the ground. I was faint from lack of food and nervous and shaking from over indulgence.

As I neared the "Chariot" I espied an old

No man can keep sound in body and mind and fill his system with alcohol.

friend, Mr. Malcolm McDowell, who furnished and superintended the distribution of the coffee and rolls. He was carefully eyeing the battered and tattered crowd as they shuffled lazily along for their little bite.

Suddenly Mr. McDowell spied me, a wreck of my former self. With an astonished and pitying look, he recognized me with a slight nod. When I had finished my "meal" and got out of the line Mr. McDowell came over, took me by the hand, and gave me a few words of friendly advice, handed me five dollars, and said: "For God's sake, Alderman, get yourself together; get out of this condition you are in, come to me when you are sober and I will assist you in any way that will rehabilitate you."

His advice was unheeded—whiskey was my master.

After leaving me Mr. McDowell walked up and down the line giving here and there "banner" (bed) money to some homeless man, speaking a

Booze is a coward when confronted by a brave man.
Alcohol, whiskey, beer, wine, all spell murder.

word to Jack or Mike, promising to secure work for others, and for several winters kept this grand humanitarian work going.

Several hungry hobos would get their bit and drop to the foot of the line and would work their way wearily back for more to eat. A repeater in a bread line is certainly hungry, and while repeaters were often discovered Mr. McDowell's orders were to turn no man away, arguing that if a man would edge his way along in the line for an hour, in the bitter cold, he certainly needed food and would be supplied.

A strapping young fellow in the line behind me, two-thirds drunk, said he had been down the line nightly and during the day "worked" everything else on "tap" for all they were worth and slept at night in the Municipal Lodging House. He said he got food during the day at the free lunches in cheap saloons and barrel houses.

The most of those in line were old, broken down men, and professional tramps and hobos of

For a sober man the battle of life is not a battle of strife. A "brain duster" puts cobwebs in your vision.

a most shiftless type. Here and there and everywhere I mixed in "with the bunch" and by their own confessions to one another and made in boasting talk to me, as the result of inquiry, they had been "bumming" around the country during the warm months, begging and stealing, but came to Chicago for the winter because as one of them put it to me: "Chicago is about the only city in the United States where things (food, etc.) come so easy and no questions asked. You can pound de sidewalks in 'Chi,' (walking the streets), night or day and de 'harness bull' (policeman) never raps." This man said he'd be off with the robins to his "country home," and back with the snowbirds to spend the cold snap in "Chi."

The law against begging and mendicancy seems to be a dead letter in Chicago. There are thousands of professional alcoholic beggars, men and boys, prowling through the city every day, wringing the dimes from a sober, sympathetic public.

A snake and a corkscrew is the fraternal badge of liquor dispensers.

MY LAST DRINK

The evils of drunkenness are known to all, and cause all this misery. Alcohol rapidly undermines the constitution, breaks down the moral character and makes complete wrecks of those who are unable to escape from its clutches. Ninety per cent of the men I encountered in the Bread Line night after night were forced there through drink. I talked and drank with hundreds of them.

It is not right for any man to derive a living from that which is debasing the minds and ruining the souls of men and forcing them into bread lines and jails. No man has a moral, or should be given a legal right to sell a poison which produces misery and madness, destroys the happiness of the domestic circle, ruins homes and families and fills the land with women and children in a far more deplorable condition than that of widows and orphans, causes nearly all the crime and pauperism that exists, and which the law abiding and sober citizenship are obliged to pay for.

A "good fellow" in a saloon is usually a brute at home. Whiskey is the most destructive agency known to man.

Saloon keepers know the goods they sell will produce these results. They are case hardened. They reason it is a legitimate business or the municipality would not legalize it by giving them a license to operate.

Every man who drinks is running the race of life with a handicap—and it is hard to win and keep a place in that race, even when one is fit and efficient.

The world has blundered dreadfully in handling the drink question. The commercialization of the alcoholic traffic and saloons, with alluring temptations on every hand, has laid a frightfully heavy tax on human vitality, efficiency, health and happiness.

Who has pity for the murderous liquor traffic? As it pleads for mercy let it remember the wrongs it has inflicted, let it remember the graves and tears of wives and mothers upon whose tender hearts its iron heel has fallen, the awful wretchedness of mind and heart of alcohol vic-

That real article of Personal Liberty, the Declaration of Independence, was not the work of the liquor interests.

tims. Let us remember how faith and love and honor and ambition have died, how soddened will has lost all power of resistance, and how the murderous greed of this iniquity has turned from the spectacle of its dead and ruined victims and reached for others who might take their place and fill its coffers. Mercy for the saloon means cruelty to mankind. Every day of grace for the saloon is a disgrace. The saloon must go utterly, must go never to return. With the saloon out of the way bread lines will automatically cease to exist.

CHAPTER ELEVEN

How Lawyers Rob and Swindle Prisoners in Jails and Courts

IN the fifty-five times I was arrested for drunkenness, disorderly conduct, passing bogus checks, securing money by false pretenses, and a dozen other crimes committed while insane from drink, no matter in what part of the world I was arrested, as soon as in the police station or jail, I was interviewed by a lawyer. If I had money, a watch or any other article of jewelry or an overcoat, he would assure me of my release. I was trapped several times into parting with what little change I had and never saw the "lawyer" again,

---

Did you ever note how the "good fellow" who treats every man in a saloon treats his family?

---

and when released could not get any information as to the identity of the shyster. No one around any police station knew anything about him, or who he was. But they knew him, just the same.

In Philadelphia I was arrested, charged with "operating a confidence game and intoxication" and I gave a lawyer $10.00 to defend me. Said he knew the judge and handed me that old bunk, "It will be all right, my boy." He stalled around and I saw at once he had no standing in the court. The judge asked me what I had to say for myself. I said I was drunk and insane. Quick as a flash the judge retorted, "I know you are drunk by your appearance and I know you are insane or you wouldn't employ this lawyer to defend you. Six months in the workhouse will sober you up and unscramble your mind."

I made an earnest plea to the judge, and so impressed him with my determination "not to take another drink" that he suspended sentence

The liquor traffic is the only black spot in the pathway of the youth of the country.

and said if I would leave the Quaker City in one hour he would discharge me. I left, went across the Delaware River to Camden, N. J., and at 5 P. M. that day was again in a cell, drunk and helpless, and the following morning I made a successful "speech" to the judge and was released, only to be picked up in Cincinnati two days later on the same charge—"disorderly conduct," drunk.

Of all the vampires, pirates and robbers the world ever knew or history records are the so-called lawyers and shysters and ambulance chasers and personal injury sharks that hang around the police stations, police courts, and hospitals, county jails, criminal and civil courts, looking for some poor devil to "defend." This is not libelling the legal profession as a whole, for any lawyer of standing or decency does not have to acquire clients in this manner. Many of these hyenas are members of the local Bar Associations in their respective cities. Nobody cares.

The courts of Chicago and all other cities

A free lunch is just a little "come along" junk, always well salted by the devil.

swarm with an army of human legal vermin who fatten upon the unfortunate, whether innocent or guilty, who fall into the clutches of the law. Every day in every police court in Chicago these "lawyers" are awaiting their victims, like so many spiders in their webs.

Every man admitted to practice at the bar in any state has legal and professional rights that permit him to visit police stations, jails and courts and fish for clients. He can take a prisoner and talk to him secretly—a "professional courtesy" the law allows a lawyer and client. Nearly every policeman in Chicago has a lawyer on his staff who is advised at once when a promising arrest is made. He is telephoned at once. These lawyers will defend you, bail you out, or do anything in the world for you if you have a little money— maybe. If an accident occurs and the wagon or ambulance is called, the first thing a policeman does is to get your name and address. The next thing is to telephone to an ambulance chasing or

Whiskey is a demon put on earth by the devil to try the souls of men.

142

personal injury lawyer. You are immediately bamboozled into signing a contract and power of attorney, and even if you have a legitimate case these hungry hyenas will settle for a small sum for the purpose of securing quick money. All hospitals have employes that give out the name, nature of accident, and address of every case that arrives. These are all well-known facts. Nobody cares. All fees received and settlements made are split three ways. The lawyer, and the informant make two—who gets the third? Somebody knows—and nobody cares!

I was locked up in the Central Police Station in La Salle Street, Chicago, along with a well-dressed Greek. He wanted his brother notified by telephone. Instead a well-known criminal lawyer came in. He gave the lawyer fifty dollars to defend him and fifty more for going on his bond for the measly sum of $300.00. He was in on some trivial charge and the next day the judge discharged him. He would have discharged him

Moderate drinking is the father of all drunkenness.
Whiskey is made in coils as a tribute to the serpent.

anyway. There was no evidence to hold him. I talked with the man later on the street and he said: "If I or my friends ever get in trouble again I will employ the same lawyer, as he has a pull." There is not a judge on the bench in the United States that pays the least attention to these pettifogging shysters.

The method of procedure in separating a prisoner from his money, diamonds, watch or any article of jewelry, or his overcoat—if it is a good one—is like this: On the way to the station the policeman who made the arrest, says: "You're in a bad jam, old top. Have you got a lawyer?" Of course not. "Well, you need a guy that can handle the judge. Just say nothing and I will send a good lawyer down to the cell to have a talk with you."

In fifteen minutes the lawyer comes.

"You have a bad case, but I can 'fix it.' Have you got any money?"

"Nothing but this diamond ring and watch,"

No man should be allowed to sell a poison which produces misery and madness.

says the party arrested, who has been picked up for some simple infraction of the law.

The lawyer claims friendship with the judge. Takes his diamond and watch; gets the case continued until his client can give him the names of eight or ten of his friends, and the lawyer will call on them with a hard luck story about the man in jail and "touch" each of them for $5 or $10. When the case is finally called the judge discharges the prisoner with a reprimand.

In nearly all police stations is a conspicuous sign, "Watch Your Step," but it ought to be changed to "Watch Your Watch."

There is something grimly grotesque with that old leaden-heeled "justice." The lead has been changed to rubber, so the lawyer crook cannot slip.

There are thousands of Chicago people who have been victims of these skinners, sharks, and shysters and today there are hundreds of lawyers practicing this robbing game and in full and hon-

The "Death Bell" on a saloon cash register is a "Death Knell."

orable professional standing. The bench and bar are fully aware of these nefarious practices. Nobody seems to care. It is somebody's business to break up this shameful system.

Frequently a lawyer who has been paid a good sum to secure bail for some one detained in a cell, will allow him to go back to jail at the request of a professional bondsman or a "bond shark," because the latter has reached the limit of his property margin and wishes to surrender the man who has already paid in order to qualify and collect from a new customer. Nobody cares!

The minute a man is arrested and haled to the police station the first thing done is to search him. Money, jewelry and all things of value are taken and you are given a receipt for same. If you are too drunk to have a complete mental inventory of your possessions you are liable to be handed a receipt for any amount, although you might have $200 in your possession. A "bond shark" and lawyer are at once notified, and when they get through, you will be thoroughly cleaned. Another favorite pastime is to run a man in for being "sassy" or failure to "move along." Search him, and if he is a live one, don't book him, but notify a "lawyer" who is on the job in a minute. He will get you out for $5 or $25, or $50, according to the amount found on your person when searched. In a few minutes you are released having never been "booked." You think the lawyer has a "pull." The police know that no judge would convict the prisoner even if booked and held. This is a favorite pastime and works particularly well at night when the commanding officer is usually at home.

A big burly copper said to me in one of the police stations:

"Alderman, the 'big fellows' are all getting theirs and we know it, and we are grabbing a bone whenever we get a chance. They are getting so bold that they will soon be tripped"— and some of them have been.

The claw of the tiger is always felt in the handshake of a liquor dealer.

MY LAST DRINK

Shortly after this conversation there were some astounding police revelations, which were only a scratch on the surface.

A poor devil gets injured and is rushed to a hospital. Out comes an ambulance chasing lawyer. Advises him to not sign any paper or settle with any claim agent. Will promise to recover $10,000 damages at once. Shows a book containing names of hundreds of men who have been injured and received award of damages. The cases are cited from every part of the United States and many are twenty years old. He claims them as his own cases and settlements.

"Just sign this power of attorney and contract and I will take your case on a contingent basis."

The poor man falls for this bunk and signs the paper. The shyster settles for little or nothing and gives his client whatever he pleases. The shyster wants quick money. Court procedure and delays do not appeal to him.

When you find a saloon keeper filled with the milk of human kindness, look out! It is usually skimmed milk.

It is well that the public should know what a "contingent fee" is. You give one of these vampires your case and he agrees to advance all court costs and fees and prosecute your case for one-half the amount received. It sounds reasonable. If the lawyer loses the suit he gets nothing; if he wins the suit you get nothing. Simple, isn't it?

Should you ever get injured or in trouble of any kind look out for the Blackstone boy with a contingent contract in his pocket.

CHAPTER TWELVE

My Coming Back

I WAGED war with the demon and I am no longer in bondage. Starting in at the scene of my defeat I am rapidly working myself up the highway of sobriety, respect, contentment and health.

It was a long, hard, bitter battle, but at last I conquered the enemy. I am now free from this terrible incubus of drink, and the memory of those ruinous years can never be wholly eradicated. My thoughts are now free from remorse or fear, for in my final rise from the cavernous depths of drunkenness and despair to the beautiful light

---

A ride in a patrol wagon is not a joy ride, but many joyous men take it.

---

of soberness and the possession of an unshackled mind I have cheerfully conveyed to the world my experience with that monster, whiskey, and to the silent and secret sufferer who has been enmeshed in the whirlpool, give encouragement, and warn drinking men of the abyss yawning to swallow and clutch and strangle them in deadly embrace unless the habit is stopped at once.

No human being or pen can truthfully portray the silent and terrible grip that gnaws at the heart of a man who is coming back to a life of sobriety after years of terrible dissipation. It is a tortuous trip. Thousands embark for passage but few arrive at an absolutely sober destination. Temptations and discouragements are always in evidence.

There is no fixed time that a man cursed and burdened with drink comes to himself, but I was coming back, and in a manner and route that proved providential. My time to be freed of the demon had been marked out. My last drunken

No one but a saloon keeper needs whiskey in his business. The drink habit is like a tornado—it grows in intensity

attempt to secure money, paradoxical as it may seem, resulted in my reformation. God certainly moves men in mysterious ways, His wonders to perform.

One cold February morning in 1914 I called at the office of the Western Fuel Company, Adams and Rockwell Streets, Chicago, and presented a check with the request that I be accommodated with the currency. While pretending to accommodate me a clerk stepped to the telephone and called up the bank whose check I was using. They told the clerk that the check was worthless, to call an officer. I heard the word "officer" repeated by the clerk to the assistant manager.

I shot out of the door, north on Rockwell Street, west on Monroe, and when I reached Washtenaw Avenue I was confronted by about twenty coal heavers from the Fuel Company's yards with shovels and clubs. Of course I surrendered. I capitulated to this vast "army." To the office I was taken. On my arrival a police

The man who wants "just one more drink" is usually an irreclaimable victim.

officer was awaiting me. I was taken to the Warren Avenue Police Station. I was trembling and nervous, shattered from drink, and the police officer took pity on my awful condition and allowed me to go into a saloon on the corner of Madison street and Campbell Avenue and secure a drink of whiskey. I was on the verge of delirium tremens. God knows I needed a stimulant. That was "My Last Drink" and from that minute I forsook strong drink forever.

The following morning I was taken to the Desplaines Street Police Station, arraigned before Judge H. P. Dolan, a jurist who had known me in the days when I was a prosperous, respected and sober citizen. As I was brought to the bar, the judge viewed me with a pitying eye and said:—"Alderman, you are charged with operating a confidence game. What have you to say?"

I admitted the charge against me was true. Told the judge I was drunk at the time, had only

The pop of a champagne cork is a warning shot of an impending battle! Look out!

a vague recollection of the transaction, that I was already on parole from Judge John P. Mahoney's court, and had just been released from the county jail. I begged the court to change the charge in the complaint from "operating a confidence game," which would send me back to the county jail to await action by the grand jury, to "disorderly conduct," which would place me within jurisdiction of his court. After some thought the judge changed the charge. I plead guilty, and was sentenced to serve sixty days in the House of Correction.

Judge Dolan was kind enough to recommend that I be placed in the hospital and requested me to write to him at the end of thirty days and if convinced I wanted to stop drinking he would assist me in securing a release. I remained in the House of Correction only a few days, however, my never failing friends coming to the front and securing my release.

After I was sentenced by the judge I was

Saloon keepers thrive by having minors form the habit of liquor drinking at the earliest possible age.

bundled into the House of Correction bus for my journey. This bus will seat about twenty, but this time it held forty human beings, packed and crowded and squeezed in. The door was locked and away we went—drunken men, Chinamen, negroes, a ragged underworld mob, and such a foul-smelling aggregation of supposedly human beings were never before huddled together. On arriving at the prison our names, ages and occupations were taken; a bath and shave followed and with a suit of prison clothes on our backs were marched to our home—a cell.

From that hour I was plunged into a profound, persistent melancholy. It was as if the whole fabric of life had suddenly toppled over and crashed down upon my brain. As I peered through the bars an awful loneliness came over me. I was sober at last. I felt such a horror at being shut out from the world that I determined that I would never touch another drop of strong

Alcohol is pushing thousands of human beings into the vortex of death.

MY LAST DRINK

drink. From that minute my coming back started. I am as firm as the Rock of Gibraltar that I have had "My Last Drink."

There was no dawn of hopefulness that I could map out. The shadows of life were lengthening and growing thinner. Time and age were relentlessly creeping and ill health, a legacy from drink, were facts whirling through my brain with lightning rapidity.

Everything was dark, dead. I realized that Time had its hand on the door of my life. There was nothing in the past to which I could turn. I must begin life over again. I flung myself on my cell cot and with closed eyes could see my past go round and round like the hands of a clock. My grief and trouble were borne in silence. The terrible quietness prevailing was worse than death itself. I was stunned. The path I had traveled had come to its end. I could not rid myself of the memory of the past. Here I was a convict. For what? For attempting to secure money in

Keep up your batting average, Mr. Boozer—the bleachers for yours.

MY LAST DRINK

an illegitimate way, to appease my insatiable desire for drink.

This same place is yawning for every drinking man. No man who flirts with alcohol is immune from the path I followed and the end I found. The clock of human life is set at a definite point. The pendulum will some day swing the other way, either for better or worse, and usually worse for the drinking man.

Coming back after you have dropped to the bottom is a slow, wearisome journey. One hardly knows which way to turn or what to do. Friends and acquaintances have lost confidence in you, employers are chary about giving employment, and I found myself at the bottom of the ladder of life. With credit, reputation and standing absolutely gone the outlook was indeed discouraging.

I soon discovered it was a pretty good world after all, for I found many loyal friends, and quickly, too.

Sober men stand, but drunken men fall in the battle of life.
A man with a shiny coat is usually a polished saloon bum.

MY LAST DRINK

To Mr. David E. Gibson, Chairman of the Mutual Improvement Committee of Oriental Consistory, and Mr. Nelson N. Lampert, Vice President of the Fort Dearborn National Bank, I owe a debt of gratitude that can never be repaid while I live, for they guided, advised and assisted me on the way to my regeneration.

As soon as I convinced these gentlemen I had taken "My Last Drink," there was nothing spared to encourage me in every way. They secured employment and tendered substantial financial assistance, exacting nothing from me but a promise to be firm. Had it not been for these two Samaritans my coming back would indeed have been rocky and almost impossible to achieve. What these good men did for me was voluntary, and they were actuated solely by a noble desire to do humanitarian work. Their mission has not been fruitless. They are as much gratified at the outcome of their kindness as myself and family.

Successful drinkers are always business failures.
A quiet drinker becomes loud with age.

MY LAST DRINK

There are scores of others in Chicago who have been restored to a life of usefulness and sobriety by these gentlemen, privately and without ostentation or publicity, men who have told me their pathetic story, and are today a credit to themselves, the community, and a pleasure to their benefactors.

If any moderate drinker who regards prohibition as an enemy to his personal liberty could only know of my happiness and contrast it with the despair I had endured through drink, surely he would not refuse to forego his moderate drink and do his utmost to put this home wrecking incubus out of reach of the poor wretches whose appetites have grown beyond their control.

Sobriety stands for law, order, peace and happiness. Whiskey stands for drunkenness, poverty, distress, crime, vice and all its countless attendant consequences.

It is not only the welfare of individuals and of families but the future of the entire nation that

Whiskey kills honesty, ambition, loyalty and all that is good in man.

is involved in this evil. It is a social, moral, religious, industrial and political question, and is vital to the future of the race as well as the nation.

Business efficiency, industrial economy, the fundamental principles of thrift, clean manhood, pure womanhood, and good citizenship, demand the abolition of the drink traffic.

The drink traffic is the paramount problem in the United States today. It constrains all citizens who believe in law and order and decency and a proper enforcement of the law to arm for the encounter, forget all party lines in the fight with a foe that is the most malignant and dangerous the world has ever known.

The rights of humanity and the good of the community must at all times first be considered, and it is my purpose to devote the remainder of my days to assist in the uplifting of those enthralled in the quagmire of drink, who have lost their moorings and are being plunged headlong into an awful maelstrom of destruction.

The rights of humanity demand the absolute overthrow of the liquor industry.

CPSIA information can be obtained
at www.ICGtesting.com
Printed in the USA
LVHW051800090123
736778LV00004B/245